A Visit to the Monastery of La Trappe in 1817

W.D. Fellowes

Contents

A VISIT TO THE MONASTERY OF LA TRAPPE IN 1817

BY

W.D. Fellowes

PREFACE.

In justice to the public and to myself, I must disavow for the following pages any higher literary pretension than what is conveyed by the simple title of "Notes," under which I have ventured to give them to the world. I had no other aim in writing but to occupy as rationally as I could the hours of travel, and no other object in publishing but to impart to others as plainly as I could a portion of the pleasure I myself experienced. It has somewhere been remarked to this effect, that if every man of common understanding were to put down the daily thoughts and occurrences of his life, candidly and unaffectedly as he experienced them, he must necessarily produce something of interest to his fellow men, and make a book, which, though not enlivened by wit, dignified by profundity of reasoning, nor valuable by extent of research, yet no man perhaps should throw aside with either weariness or disgust.

Whether I shall prove fortunate enough not to excite these sensations in such readers as may honour my book with a perusal, I fear to conjecture. But it was my good fortune, during a season of uncommon beauty, to make a tour through some of the most interesting parts of France, and to meet with persons who, from situation and talents, were highly calculated to give my journey every charm of society and information. The natural face of the country through which I passed was peculiarly beautiful: I could scarcely move a step without some novelty of picturesque enchantment, and had the most perfect opportunities of contemplating Nature in all her varied poetry, from the grand and terrible graces of savage sublimity, to the soft and playful loveliness of cultivated luxuriance. There was scarcely a town or village where I arrived which romance or history, religion or politics, had not invested and adorned with every interest of mental association. Under such impressions, and with such opportunities, it was scarcely possible to resist recording something of what I saw and felt; and if the publication of my hasty record be an error, it will be deemed by my friends, I hope, a pardonable one. My book can scarcely demand the serious attention of the critic; nor could criticism well expect a better style from one whose profession is seldom supposed to allow much leisure to acquire nicety in the arts of composition. I claim no other merit for my Notes than having followed the advice (of Gray, I believe) that ten words put down at the moment upon the spot, are worth a whole cart load of recollections. I have not sought to add to their attraction (if they should possess any) by the embellishments of my invention, or the graces of my periods--the decorative artifices of execution can never give value to falsehood, and truth needs them not. A simple landscape, simply described from nature, has always a charm above the most high-finished compositions of mere fancy; and, like a moderate painting from the same source, still imparts a feeling of reality. I hope, therefore, I shall be excused for attempting some description, slight and unskilful as it may be, of places and scenery where the human mind has exhibited some of its most curious and powerful features, and which awaken reflections of the deepest interest--I allude particularly to the monastery of *La Trappe*, and to the country of *La Vendee*. The former had dwelt among the earliest impressions of youth, with something like the wild and wonderful force of a romantic tale; and I was anxious to become an eye-witness of what had so long been one of the most powerful objects of my imagination. The gloomy and almost inaccessible situation chosen by this strange fraternity for their convent--their rigid separation from human intercourse--the infringible taciturnity imposed upon themselves--and the terrible severity of their penances, are certainly circumstances more resembling the visionary indulgence of fantasy and fiction, than actual realities to be met with among living men, and in the present day.

With regard to the department of *La Vendee*, whatever serves, trivial as it may be, to recall or illustrate the history of its wars and the character of its inhabitants, must ever possess a charm for those who delight to sympathize with the noble struggles of a gallant people, conscientiously devoting themselves to the cause of a fallen and persecuted monarchy, and resisting the cruel and destructive ferocity of a licentious enemy, who had broken down the most sacred fences of society, and trampled upon the dearest ties of human nature.

In these Notes, slight as they are, I can truly promise the reader that he will find nothing wilfully misrepresented, nor advanced without just authority; and if the rapid and cursory character of the observations, allusions, and anecdotes, shall enable an hour to pass agreeably that has no better employment, I am content, and gratified with the attainment of all I ever hoped or designed by an unpretending publication, which I cheerfully dedicate to all who love to unbend their minds from a critical attitude, and can lounge goodnaturedly over leaves written by a traveller as idle and careless as themselves, and who assures them that no one can think more humbly of his production than himself.

MARCH 1818.

CHAP. I.

ROUTE FROM PARIS TO MORTAGNE.--EXCURSION TO LA TRAPPE.--STATE OF THE ORDER SINCE THE RESTORATION IN 1814.--ITS FOUNDATION AND RULES UNDER THE ABBE DE RANCE.

I performed this journey during the months of June, July, August, and September, a distance of near one thousand miles, and had the singular good fortune to enjoy the finest weather possible. The perusal of Madame de La Roche-Jaquelin's interesting work on the Vendean war, first gave me the idea of visiting the country called le Bocage, the theatre of so many events, and sufferings of the brave royalists; and, as the province of le Perche, in which is situated the ancient convent of La Trappe, was in my route to Bretagne, I resolved to make an excursion there, in order to satisfy myself of the truth of those austerities which I had read of in the Memoirs of the Count de Comminge.

The route from Paris to Mortagne, in le Perche, leads through Marly, Versailles, Saint Cyr, Pont Chartrain, La Queue, Houdon, Marrolles, Dreux, Nonancourt, Tillieres, Verneuil, and Saint Maurice. The roads are excellent, and the country beautiful. The first post out of Paris is Nanterre. Two leagues and a half from the barriere, the village of Ruel, and the park of Malmaison, form a continuation of neat buildings. At Nanterre, in the campaign of 1815, the Prussians, after a severe engagement with the retreating troops of the French, had one regiment of cavalry cut to pieces. At Ruel, the celebrated Cardinal Richelieu had a palace, which at the Revolution became national property, and was purchased by Massena, Duc de Rivoli, Prince D'Essling, lately deceased. The Duchess still resides there. It was taken possession of by the allies in 1815, and, like Malmaison, plundered by the troops. There are extensive barracks for cavalry at this place, at present occupied by the Swiss guards.

A little farther, between Malmaison and Marly, is a beautiful chateau, formerly belonging to General Count Bertrand, who accompanied Napoleon to Saint Helena; it is now the property of M. Ouverard, the banker: nearly opposite is the residence of the celebrated Abbe Sieyes, who lives in great retirement. Whatever may have been the political transgressions of Bertrand, there is something so noble in his devotion to the fallen fortunes of his master, that it is impossible not to respect his character.

At Marly, the water-works and aqueduct for conveying the water from the river Seine to the palace and gardens of Versailles, are very curious. The palace of Marly is destroyed; but the basins, which were constructed by order of Louis XIV. are still to be seen, though in ruins. Delille, the poet, in his description of the chateau and beautiful grounds of Marly, says:

C'est la que tout est grand, que l'art n'est point timide;
La tout est enchante: c'est le Palais d'Armide;
C'est le jardin d'Alcine, ou plutot d'un Heros,
Noble dans sa retraite et grand dans son repos.
Qui cherche encore a vaincre, a dompter des obstacles,
Et ne marche jamais qu'entoure de miracles.

On quitting Paris, I had procured a letter of introduction from Count La Cou to Madame de Bellou, at Mortagne, a charming old lady of an ancient and noble family in that province, who had never quitted the seat of her ancestors, but remained quiet and respected during all the storms of the revolution. She received me with kindness, and politely introduced me to the Sub-Prefect, Monsieur Lamorelie, who gave me a letter of introduction to the Pere Don Augustin, Grand Prior of La Trappe. The mayor of the commune of Solignie, who happened to be at the inn, and learned from the ***Aubergiste***, that a stranger intended visiting La Trappe, very civilly introduced himself to me, and gave me every necessary direction how to proceed through the forest; at the same time expressing his surprise that an Englishman should take the trouble, and undergo the fatigue of penetrating through such a country, an attempt which few of his own countrymen had ever ventured to make. It was singular enough that only one person in the town could be found to accompany me as a guide, or who knew any thing of the track through the forest, although the abbey is distant only twenty-five miles.

I set out with the guide just at day-break, mounted on a small Norman horse, and armed with pistols and a sword-cane, in case of meeting with wolves, which the mayor of Solignie had cautioned me against, as abounding throughout the country. We travelled, after leaving the main road, at the distance of a league, through a country scarcely appearing to be inhabited. Here and there a lone cot, a mere speck, met the eye amidst a landscape composed of nothing but barren wastes and thick forests, nearly impervious to the light. We had penetrated about half a mile through one of the latter, my attention occupied with the romantic wildness of the scene, when we were alarmed by the howling of a wolf. My guide crossed himself, and began cracking his whip with the noise and singular dexterity peculiar to the French postillions; and as we entered a part of the forest, impenetrable but for traces known only to those who are accustomed to them, he related (by way of consolation, I suppose,) several stories of the peasantry having been recently attacked, and some destroyed, by wolves; and one instance of a woman having had her infant torn from her arms, only a short time since, in the neighbourhood.

On quitting the forest the track was now and then diversified by the ruins of a solitary cottage, or the mouldering remains of a crucifix, raised by pious hands to mark some event, or to guide the traveller; and after traversing a rocky plain, covered with heath and wild thyme, where some herds of sheep and goats were browsing, attended by the shepherd, we entered the Forest of Bellegarde. This forest spreads over a large extent of country, and is so dark and intricate, that those best acquainted with it frequently lose their way. No vestige of human footsteps or of the track of animals appeared; a mark, here and there, on some of the trees, was the only direction! Pursuing our way through turnings and windings the most perplexing, we found ourselves to be on the overhanging brow of a hill, the descent of which was so precipitous, that we were under the necessity of dismounting; and by a winding path, hollowed out in its side, descended through a sort of labyrinth towards the valley, whose sides were clothed with lofty woods, rising one above the other. The valley itself is interspersed with three lakes, connected with each other, and forming a sort of moat around the ground; in the centre of which appears the venerable abbey of La Trappe, with its dark gray towers, the deep tone of whose bell had previously announced to us, that we had nearly reached our journey's end.

The situation of this monastery was well adapted to the founder's views, and to suggest the name it originally received of La Trappe, from the intricacy of the road which descends to it, and the difficulty of access or egress, which exists even to this day, though the woods have been very much thinned since the revolution. Perhaps there never was any thing in the whole universe better calculated to inspire religious awe than the first view of this monastery. It was imposing even to breathlessness. The total solitude--the undisturbed and chilling silence, which seem to have ever slept over the dark and ancient woods--the still lakes, reflecting the deep solemnity of the objects around them--all impress a powerful image of utter seclusion and hopeless separation from living man, and appear formed at once to court and gratify the sternest austerities of devotion--to nurse the fanaticism of diseased imaginations--to humour the wildest fancies--and promote the gloomiest schemes of penance and privation!

In descending the steep and intricate path the traveller frequently loses sight of the abbey, until he has actually reached the bottom; then emerging from the wood, the following inscription is seen carved on a wooden cross:

> C'est ici que la mort et que la verite
> Elevent leurs flambeaux terribles;
> C'est de cette demeure, au monde inaccessible,
> Que l'on passe a l'eternite.

A venerable grove of oak trees, which formerly surrounded the monastery, was cut down in the revolution. In the gateway of the outer court is a statue of Saint Bernard, which has been mutilated by the republicans: he is holding in one hand a church, and in the other a spade--the emblems of devotion and labour. This gateway leads into a court, which opens into a second enclosure, and around that are the granaries, stables, bakehouse, and other offices necessary to the abbey, which have all been happily preserved.

Owing to the fatigue of the journey, the heat of the weather, and having frequently been obliged to retrace our steps, from losing our way in the woods, it was late before we arrived at the abbey. To the west, under the glow of the setting sun, the forests were still tinged with the warmest yet softest colours that faded fast away; and as we descended towards the Convent, quickening our pace to reach it before the last gleams of evening departed, there was a silence around us, which at such a moment, and in such a spot, sunk sorrowfully upon the heart! Just as I reached the gate the bell tolled in so solemn and melancholy a tone that it vibrated through my whole frame, and called strongly to mind the beautiful lines in "Parisina":

> The Convent bells are ringing,
> But mournfully and slow;
> In the gray square turret swinging,
> With a deep sound, to and fro,
> Heavily to the heart they go!

On entering the gate, a lay-brother received me on his knees; and in a low and whispering voice informed me they were at vespers. The stillness and gloom of the building--the last rays of the sun scarcely penetrating through its windows--the deep tones of the monks chanting the responses, which occasionally broke the silence, filled me with reverential emotions which I felt unwilling to disturb: it was necessary however to present my letter of introduction, and Frere Charle, the secretaire, soon after came out, and received me with great civility. He appeared a young man about five-and-twenty, with a handsome and prepossessing countenance. He informed me that the Pere Abbe was then absent, visiting a convent of Female Trappistes, a few leagues distant, but that he should be happy to show me every attention; and requested that in going over the Convent, I would neither speak nor ask him any questions in those places where I saw him kneel, or in the presence of any of the Monks. I followed him to the chapel, where, as soon as the service was over, the bell rung to summon them to supper. Ranged in double rows, with their heads enveloped in a large cowl, and bent down to the earth, they chanted the grace, and then seated themselves. During the repast one of them, standing, read passages from scripture, reminding them of death, and of the shortness of human existence; another went round the whole community, and on his knees kissed their feet in succession, throwing himself prostrate on the floor at intervals before the image of our Saviour; a third remained on his knees the whole time, and in that attitude took his repast. These penitents had committed some fault, or neglected their religious duties, of which, according to the regulations, they had accused themselves, and were in consequence doomed to the above modes of penance.

The refectory was furnished with long wooden tables and benches; each person was provided with a trencher, a jug of water, and a cup, having on it the name of the brother to whom it is appropriated, as Frere Paul, Frere Francois, &c. which name they assume on taking the vow. Their supper consisted of bread soaked in water, a little salt, and two raw carrots, placed by each; water alone is their beverage. The dinner is varied with a little cabbage or other vegetables: they very rarely have cheese, and never meat, fish, or eggs. The bread is of the coarsest kind possible.

Their bed is a small truckle, boarded, with a single covering, generally a blanket, no mattress nor pillow; and, as in the former time, no fire is allowed but one in the great hall, which they never approach.

Within these three years a small cabaret has been built near the Convent for the accommodation of those who may occasionally visit it, the buildings that remain being but barely sufficient for their own members, which have been rapidly increasing since its restoration. In this cabaret I took up my abode for the night, in preference to the accommodation very kindly offered me by Frere Charle, and retired to rest, wearied with the day's excursion, and fully satisfied, that all I had heard, all I had imagined of La Trappe, was infinitely short of the reality, and that no adequate description could be given of its awful and dreary solitude;

Monsieur Elzear de Sabran, in a poem called Le Repentir, lately published, describing this Monastery, says very justly;

Temoins d'une commune et secrete souffrance,
Ces freres de douleur, martyrs de l'esperance,
D'une lente torture epuisant les degres,
Constamment reunis, constamment separes,
L'un a l'autre etrangers, a cote l'un de l'autre,
Joignent tout ce malheur encore a tout le notre,
Jamais, dans ses pareils cherchant un tendre appui,
Un coeur ne s'ouvre aux coeurs qui souffrent comme lui.

The following morning the matin bell summoned me to the Convent, and Frere Charle attended me to the burial ground; here have been deposited the remains of two of the brothers, deceased since the restoration of their order in 1814. Another grave was ready prepared; as soon as an interment takes place, one being always opened for the next that may die. The two graves were marked with simple wooden crosses, bearing the following inscriptions:

F. Nicolas. Frere DONNE
Decede. le 24 Fevrier 1816.

*   *   *   *   *

On the other:

F. AUGUSTINUS. NOVITIUS
die 26 mensis novembris
ANNO. 1816 DECESSIT.
REQUIESCAT IN PACE
AMEN.

*   *   *   *   *

In the centre of the cemetery is the grave of M. De Rance. His monument, with his figure carved at full length in a recumbent posture, was removed when the destruction of the old church took place; it is now a complete ruin, and a few stones alone mark the spot of its ancient founder's grave, which is kept free from weeds with pious reverence and care. The revolution, which like a torrent swept all before it, did not even spare the dead.

While I was contemplating the ruins around me, and watching the motions of a venerable figure in silent prayer at one of the angles, the bell tolled, when both Frere Charle and the Monk dropped instantly on their knees. How forcibly were the following lines of Pope recalled to my mind!

Lo, the struck deer, in some sequester'd part,
Lies down to die, (the arrow in his heart;)
There, hid in shades, and wasting day by day,
Inly he bleeds, and pants his soul away.

The number of Monks who have taken the vow are not in proportion to the others, who are lay brothers, and *Freres Donnes*; in all there are about one hundred, besides novices, who are principally composed of boys, and who do not wear the same habit. The Trappistes, who compose the first order, are clothed in dark brown, with brown mantle and hood; the others are in white, with brown mantle and hood. I occasionally caught a glimpse of their faces, but it was only momentarily; and I can easily believe, with their perpetual silence, that two people well known to each other, might inhabit the same spot, without ever being aware of it, so completely are their faces hidden by their large cowl. The Trappistes, or first order, are distinguished by the appellation of *Freres Convers*, the others by that of *Religieux de Coeur*.

The hardships undergone by these monks appear almost insupportable to human nature, and notwithstanding the immense number of deaths occasioned by their rigorous austerities, the Cenobites of La Trappe, at the suppression of their order, amounted to one hundred monks, sixty-nine lay brothers, and fifty-six *Freres Donnes*. The inmates are classed under these three heads; but the lay brothers, who take the same vows, and follow the same rules, are principally employed as servants, and in transacting the temporal concerns of the abbey. The *Freres Donnes* are brothers given for a time; these last are not properly belonging to the order, they are rather, religious persons, whose business or connexions prevent their joining the order absolutely, but, who wishing to renew serious impressions, or to retire from the world for a given period, come here and conform strictly to the regulations while they remain, without wishing to join the order for life. Many persons on their first conversion, or after some peculiar dispensations of Providence, retire here for a season.

In the refectory I observed a board hung up, with "*Table pour l'Office Divin*," written over it, and under it the regulations or order of service to be performed for that week, which are occasionally varied, but never diminished in their rigour.

Frere Charle said, that the whole were strictly observed, and were frequently much more severe; for the Pere Abbe had instituted more austere regulations than formerly, with the only one exception, of the sick being allowed medicines; and, in cases of great debility, a small quantity of meat.

The Table "*pour l'Office Divin*," was as follows.

Dimanche....12 Lecons et Communion.
Lundi....... 3 Lecons.
Mardi.......12 Lecons--a jeun--Travail.
Mercredi....12 Lecons.
Jeudi....... 3 Lecons.
Vendredi....12 Lecons--a jeun--Travail.
Samedi......12 Lecons--a jeun--Travail.

Their mode of life and regulations exist nearly in the same state as established by the founder; in reciting them, such horrible perversions of human nature and reason make it almost difficult to believe the existence of so severe an order, and lead us to wonder at the artificial miseries, which the ingenuity of pious but morbid enthusiasm can inflict upon itself. The abstinence practised at La Trappe allows not the use of meat, fish, eggs, or butter; and a very limited quantity of bread and vegetables. They only eat twice a day; which meals consist of a slender repast at about eleven in the morning, and two ounces of bread and two raw carrots in the evening: both together do not at any time exceed twelve ounces. The same spirit of mortification is observable in their cells, which are very small, and have no other furniture than a bed of boards, a human skull, and a few religious books.

Silence is at all times rigidly maintained; conversation is never permitted: should two of them even be seen standing near each other, though pursuing their daily labour, and preserving the strictest silence, it is considered as a violation of their vow, and highly criminal; each member is therefore as completely insulated as if he alone existed in the Monastery. None but the Pere Abbe knows the name, age, rank, or even the native country of any member of the community: every one, at his first entrance, assumes another name, as I before observed, and with his former appellation, each is supposed to abjure, not only the world, but every recollection and memorial of himself and connexions: no word ever escapes from his lips by which the others can possibly guess who he is, or where he comes from; and persons of the same name, family, and neighbourhood, have often lived together in the Convent for years, unknown to each other, without having suspected their proximity.

The abstraction of mind practised at La Trappe, and the prevention of all external communication with the world is such, that few but the superior know any thing of what is passing in it. It has been related, that so little information of the affairs of mankind did these people receive, that the death of Louis XIV. was not known there for years, except by the Father Abbe; and such was their state of seclusion, that a Nobleman having taken a journey of five hundred miles, purposely to see the Monastery, could scarcely find in the neighbouring villages one person who knew where it was situated. Indeed, at the present day, it is quite astonishing how little is known of this place, and how very few, even among those in its immediate vicinity, have ever visited it.[1]

On the great festivals they rise at midnight; otherwise they are not called until three quarters past one: at two they assemble in the Chapel, where they perform different services, public and private, until seven in the morning, according to the regulations of the week, as exemplified in the "*Table pour l'Office Divin*". At this hour they go out to labour in the open air. Their work is of the most fatiguing kind, is never intermitted, winter or summer, and admits of no relaxation from the state of the weather.

When their labour is over, they go into Chapel for a short time, until eleven o'clock, the hour of repast; at a quarter after eleven they read till noon; and afterwards lie down to rest for an hour: they are then summoned into the garden, where they again work until three; then read again for three quarters of an hour, and retire for another quarter to their private meditations, by way of preparation for vespers, which begin at four, and end at six; at seven they again enter the Chapel, and at eight they leave it, and retire to rest.

At the hour of their first repast, I again attended Frere Charle to the eating-room, where nearly the same forms were observed as at their evening-meal; a small basin of boiled cabbage, two raw carrots, and a small piece of black bread, with a

---

1   Among the most frequent visitors of La Trappe, was the unfortunate James the Second. His first visit was on the 20th November, 1690, where he was received by M. de Rance, whose account of it is very interesting.

jug of water, constituted their solitary meal. A Monk, during the whole time, read sentences from Scripture; and a small hand-bell filled up the intervals of his silence, and proclaimed a cessation from eating, or movement of any sort. Over the door of the Refectory I observed the following inscription in Latin:--"Better is a dinner of herbs, where love is, than a stalled ox, and hatred therewith".

Frere Charle invited me to partake of the frugal fare of his order. He said, "You will forgive my laying before you a vegetable repast; it is all that I have in my power to offer you, but you will confer a pleasure by accepting it". It was impossible to refuse, for I felt I should appear ungrateful after the attentions that had been shown me, if I had. Frere Charle conducted me into an apartment, in which I was gratified to observe a well executed portrait of the Abbe de Rance, which, at the destruction of the Monastery, had been preserved by the surgeon of the ancient fraternity, who continued to reside there until the period of his death, four or five years since. This person was greatly respected by all the people round the country, and resorted to by all who sought relief either from sickness or misery!--Had the other brothers followed his example of remaining, in all probability their Convent might have been spared, for the accumulation of wealth could not be laid to their charge; and as their monastic vows obliged them to remain within the Monastery, they were most unlikely to incur the suspicion of any political intrigues.--How indeed could men, whose whole existence was passed in solitude and penance, and who never conversed even among themselves, have been dangerous to those turbulent spirits who had overturned the government and all the religious institutions of their country!

In the portrait, the Abbe is dressed in the habit of the order, a white gown and hood, and sitting with a book before him, in which he appears to be writing; on the same table, before him, are a crucifix and a skull. The following inscription is painted in one corner by the artist:

"ARM'D. LE BOUTTHILLIER DE RANCE. S'R
SCAUANT. et celebre Abbe Reformateur De La Trappe.
Mort en 1700. a pres de 77 ans, et de 40 ans de la plus
austere penitence".

The Monastery of La Trappe is one of the most ancient Abbeys of the order of

Benedictins: it was established under the pontificate of Innocent the Second, during the reign of Louis VII. in the year 1140, by Rotrou, the second Count of Perche, and is said to have been built to accomplish a vow, made in the peril of shipwreck. In commemoration of this circumstance, the roof was made in the shape of the bottom of a ship inverted. It was founded under the auspices of Saint Bernard, the first Abbot of Clairvaux, the celebrated preacher in favour of the Crusades. Many ages, however, had elapsed, since its first institution, when the Father Abbot de Rance, the celebrated reformer of his time, determined to become a member, whose singular history and conversion was the subject of a poem by Monsieur Barthe.

The Abbe de Rance became a Monk of the Benedictin order of La Trappe, in 1660, and his conversion was attributed to a lady whom he tenderly loved. They had been separated for some time by her parents; she having written to him to remove her for the purpose of becoming united in marriage, he set off, but, during his journey, she was seized with a fever and died. Totally ignorant of the circumstance, he approached the house under cover of the night, and got into her apartment through the window. The first object he beheld was the coffin which contained the body of his beloved mistress! It had been made of lead, but being found to be too short, they had, with unheard of brutality; severed her head from her body! Horror-struck with the shocking spectacle, he, from that hour, renounced all connexion with the world, and imposed upon himself the most rigid austerities, which he continued until his death, forty years after.

When M. de Rance undertook the superintendance of the Monastery, it exhibited a melancholy picture, of the greatest declension, and it is curious to peruse the steps by which he effected so wonderful a change;[2] and how men could ever feel it either an inclination or a duty to enter upon a mode of life so different from the common ways of thinking or feeling.

The Monks of La Trappe were not only immersed in luxury and sloth, but were abandoned to the most scandalous excesses; most of them lived by robbery, and several had committed assassinations on the travellers who had occasion to traverse the woods. The neighbourhood shrunk with terror from the approach of men who never went abroad unarmed, and whose excursions were marked with bloodshed and violence. The Banditti of La Trappe was the appellation by which

2   Reglements de L'Abbaye, La Maison-Dieu Notre Dame de La Trappe, par Dom. Armand de Rance.

they were most generally distinguished. Such were the men amongst whom M. de Rance resolved to fix his abode; all his friends endeavouring to dissuade him from an undertaking, they deemed alike hopeless and dangerous.

"Unarmed, and unassisted,"[3] says his historian, "but in the panoply of God, and by his Spirit, he went alone amidst this company of ruffians, every one of whom was bent on his destruction. With undaunted boldness, he began by proposing the strictest reform, and not counting his life dear to him, he described the full intent of his purpose, and left them no choice but obedience or Expulsion".

"Many were the dangers M. de Rance underwent; plans were laid, at various times, to poison him, to waylay and assassinate him, and even once one of his monks shot at him; but the pistol, which was applied close to his head, flashed in the pan, and missed fire. By the good providence of God all these plans were frustrated, and M. de Rance not only brought his reform to bear, but several of his most violent persecutors became his most stedfast adherents; many were, after a short time, won over by his piety--the rest left the Monastery. He especially, who had shot at M. de Rance, became eminently distinguished for his piety and learning, and was afterwards Sub-Prior of La Trappe".

M. de Rance lived forty years at the head of this singular society, and the same ardor and piety continued to distinguish him to the last. The excess of self-denial and discipline, exercised by this order, which might readily be doubted, became more known, especially to this country, at the time of the French Revolution, when they shared the fate of dissolution with the various religious orders in France. On that occasion many of them sought an asylum in England, and were settled in Dorsetshire, where they received the kind protection and benevolent assistance of Mr. Weld, until the restoration enabled most of them to return; and, surprising as it may appear in the present age, notwithstanding the perpetual violence imposed by their regulations on every human feeling, many are found anxious to enter the establishment.

When I was about to take my leave of Frere Charle, he said, "he hoped I was pleased with my humble fare: to such as it was I had been truly welcome". Indeed he had treated me with the kindest, most unaffected hospitality; he had laid the

---

3 The work from which I have taken this, is a translation by Mrs. Schimmelpenninck of Dom. Claude Lancelot's Narrative, published in 1667. The present regulations not differing from the former, I have extracted some of the most important.

table, spread the dishes before me, stood the whole time by the side of my chair, and pressed me to eat: How could I not be thankful? I requested he would be seated, but he observed that it was not proper for him to be so. His manners and general deportment bespoke him a well-bred gentleman; and when I ventured to ask if I might make a memorandum of his name, he bowed his head with meekness and resignation, and said, "I have now no other but that which was bestowed on me when I took the vow, which severs me from the world for ever!" It was impossible not to be affected at the manner and tone of voice in which he uttered this. When I said that perhaps he would like that I should leave an acknowledgment in writing, expressive of the gratitude I felt at my kind and hospitable reception, he appeared much pleased, and instantly procured me paper. I left with him the following lines:

"Convent of La Trappe, July 20, 1817.

"I have this day visited the Convent of La Trappe,
and in the absence of the Grand Prior, to whom I
brought a letter of introduction from Monsieur Lamorelie,
Sub-Prefect of Mortagne, I was received and
have been entertained by Frere Charle Marie, his Secretary.

"It is quite impossible that I can do justice to the
kind, polite, and hospitable reception I have met with
from him, by any expressions in writing. I can only
observe, that it has made an impression on my mind
never to be effaced! If these worthy and pious people
have abandoned the world for the solitude and austerities
of La Trappe, they have not forgotten, in their own self-denial,
the benevolence and benignity due to strangers.
May their self-devotion meet with its reward!"

I now took my leave of the Convent with feelings which I will not pretend to describe, but which, together with the impressions I received when I first entered it, and the whole circumstances of my visit, I am conscious of retaining while "Memory holds her seat". The following lines, by P. Mandard, on quitting La Trappe, convey a very faithful and poetical picture of this extraordinary solitude:

  --Saint desert, sejour pur et paisible,
Solitude profonde, au vice inaccessible;
Impetueux torrens, et vous sombres forets,
Recevez mes adieux, comme aussi mes regrets!
Toujours epris de vous, respectable retraite,
Puisse-je, dans le cours d'une vie inquiete,
Dans ce flux eternel de folie et d'erreur,
Ou flotte tristement notre malheureux coeur;
Puisse-je, pour charmer mes ennuis et mes peines,
Souvent fuir en esprit au bord de vos fontaines,
Egarer ma pensee au milieu de vos bois,
Par un doux souvenir rappeler mille fois
De vos Saints habitans les touchantes images,
Penetrer, sur leurs pas, dans vos grottes sauvages,
Me placer sur vos monts, et la, prennant l'essort,
Aller chercher en Dieu ma joie, et mon tresor!

CHAP. II.

VAL-DIEU.--RUINS OF THE CONVENT OF THE CHARTREUSE.--FOR-
ESTS OF LE PERCHE, MORTAGNE.

I quitted *La Trappe* in the afternoon of the third day after my arrival there, for the Val-Dieu, which lies three leagues to the east of Mortagne, taking the villages of Rinrolles and Prepotin in my way; the latter stands in the midst of a forest. By this road, so bad that it scarcely deserves the name, a great distance is saved, but the romantic scenery of the approach to La Trappe is lost. The one we took through the forest of Bellegarde more than doubles the distance; but the Abbey is seen as in the centre of a lake beneath, and the continual beauty and wildness of the landscape render it far preferable. Until the Revolution this was the only road, the other having been made when the lands became national property, and were sold to the peasantry.

After passing through the above villages, we came round by Tourouvre, a village on a height, which has a manufactory for glass. I did not stop to view it, having several leagues to go through a wooded country. Soon after crossing the main road leading into Bretagne, we rode by the side of cultivated lands and orchards resembling the western parts of Devonshire, of which the narrow lanes and high hedges reminded me very much, until we entered the forest leading to the Val-Dieu. Between eight and nine in the evening we came to the edge bounding that part of the Vale by which it is approached, in the direction we had taken. It was very considerably out of our way, owing to the guide having mistaken his road and turned to the left instead of the right. After resting a few minutes on the brow of the hill, we began our descent by a steep and narrow pathway. When we were midway down the glen, the ruins of the ancient Chartreuse suddenly burst upon the view! At this moment all the terrors of the declivity, and the momentary expectation of meeting some of the wolves with which the forest abounds, vanished from my mind before the feelings of delight which the enchanting scene called forth. The almost perpendicular view of the Vale beneath, had an effect tremendous yet pleasing: on the left was a lake, seeming to encircle an ancient convent embosomed in a wood; a thick forest covered the surrounding heights, and before me stood the remains of the ancient Priory, with its gateway and lodge so perfect as to create no suspicion of the destruction within.

This had been the hottest day and finest weather I had experienced during my journey. It was a sweet evening, and the rich tints of the departing sun-beams among the woods, with the solitary calmness of the scenery around, were circumstances that made a strong impression on my feelings. Those who have never traversed the forests of this country can form but a very imperfect idea of what they are, or of the death-like awful stillness that reigns within them; for many miles together they form a dense shade, which, like a dark awning, completely conceals the sun from the view: even on the brightest day the sun's rays are only visible as from the bottom of a deep well! The forests in Le Perche are reckoned the most extensive in France, and every where abound with vast quantities of game.

I was received on alighting from my horse by a M. Boderie, a good humoured hospitable man, who, with his family, are the only inhabitants of this lonesome spot. I found afterwards that he had seen better days: he informed me the Val-Dieu property was purchased at the dissolution of the Monastery by the present proprietor, who resided at Paris, and allowed him, being his friend, to occupy that part of the building which had not been destroyed. He made many apologies for the badness of the accommodations and the homeliness of the fare he had to offer me, which I considered as unnecessary, as what he possessed was tendered with unaffected cheerfulness.

The Prussians in 1815 occupied this country, and notwithstanding M. Boderie was absent at that time serving in the body guard of Louis XVIII, whom he had accompanied in his retreat to Ghent, they plundered him of every article, not even leaving his wife a change of linen. The numerous accounts I have heard from people of respectability and loyalty, of the treatment experienced from the Prussians, excites the greatest regret that they were not able to distinguish the innocent from the guilty. Many families have been ruined, or greatly distressed in their circumstances who were devoted to the cause of their Sovereign. Such are the inevitable consequences of war!

The Val-Dieu extends upwards of three miles in length, surrounded by almost impenetrable woods, except where paths have been cut. It has three lakes, one communicating with the other, containing great quantities of fish. The Monastery, it is evident from the remains of its ruins, and from the boundary wall, still entire, must have been of prodigious extent. M. Boderie informed me, that the plan, of which he had seen an engraving, showed it to have been one of the most considerable in the kingdom: some idea may be formed of its former celebrity and extent by the remains of six hundred fire-places being still traceable. A colonnade surrounded the whole, forming an oblong square, in the centre of which was a jet d'eau, with several smaller ones, the basins of which are still to be seen; the space within formed a garden, with delicious walks, resembling those in the Palais Royal.

The gate-way remains perfect, excepting only that the images over the side doors have been mutilated. The one in the centre (over the great entrance) is still in excellent preservation, and appears to be finely executed: it is the figure of the Virgin Mary in gray marble, the size of life, seated, with the infant Jesus in her arms. On a scroll beneath are these letters:--

ECCE MATER
TVA.
1760.

Several old chesnut trees and elms still remain, which once formed a fine avenue in front of the building, from whence the prospect is strikingly beautiful. The eye passes over rocks, rugged, broken, and abrupt towards their summits, crowned and darkened with wood; and the narrow road winding between the trees, until it loses itself in the forest, forms a feature very gratifying to the traveller. The solitude of the place, as I viewed it at the close of day, occasioned mingled sensations of pleasure and pain. It was impossible to resist the imposing power of a situation, where every natural object was deeply tinged with the poetical character, and every remnant of architecture associated with the romance of religious feeling. I recalled and dwelt upon various passages of the poets inspired by similar scenes, and thought of the holy and enthusiastic minds which had here devoted themselves to the sublimest duties and severest sacrifices of the altar; and felt, that had I lived in those days, I, perhaps, could have become an inmate of walls which seem to have been erected to exclude the evils of life, and to nurture only the enchanting abstractions of unpolluted virtue and happiness: but the present day has brought with it a general philosophy and knowledge of human nature, which lessen the delight of contemplating the calm repose of such a seclusion, and have taught that these retreats from the world were not always retreats from vice; that the sacrifices of monkish privacy were not always those of selfish feelings; and that the austerities once practised here, as now at La Trappe, might perhaps arise more frequently from disappointed pride and ambition, than from the pure feelings of pious resignation. In the overthrow of the monarchy and that of the priesthood, this venerable pile became the object of popular vengeance; and had the Revolution done no more than effected the dissolution of the different orders of monks and nuns, every reflecting mind must have been pleased: the removal of those abuses, like the division of landed property into smaller portions, (whereby the country in general became more cultivated and productive,) was serviceable to France; and, if any circumstance can restore permanent tranquillity, it will be the interest which the different landholders have in the soil and the representative system, which will serve to check the ambition of its future governors. Already the good effects of these are to be perceived; and the excessive abuses, insolence, and profligacy, of ancient ministerial oppression, which paved the way for the downfall of the monarchy, and, like a pestilence, destroyed that which was good with that which was evil, will be prevented in future.

It is, nevertheless, melancholy to observe the traces of devastation visible in all directions: the people themselves appear not to regard it, but this may arise partly from the long and habitual feelings generated by the scenes to which the Revolution daily gave rise, and partly from the constitutional cheerfulness of the natives, who seldom view objects through the same dark medium that ours are supposed to do, and who, though they are not celebrated for patience, are of all mankind the least liable to despondency. When I spoke to M. Boderie of my regret at the destruction of an ancient structure like the one in question, his answer was, immediately, "oui c'est bien malheureux; mais enfin que voulez-vous?" He was "desole" or had "le coeur tres sensible a tout cela;" but finished by "il faut se consoler". With this sort of philosophy they are always ready to view the past, and accept of consolation, and in amusement, seek to bear or dissipate the calamities inseparable from such a state of events, without even appearing to repine. None of them will ever enter into conversation on the subject if it can be avoided.

The following day, having taken leave of my hospitable host, who refused any compensation, I returned to Mortagne by another route, through the Forest of Val-Dieu, more dark and difficult to penetrate than the other; but the guide was better acquainted with it, and took the road by Saint Maure and Saint Eloi, through a fine country, highly cultivated, and abounding in beautiful scenery and distant landscapes. It was late at night before I reached Mortagne, greatly fatigued from the excessive heat of the weather.

I dined the following day with Madame de Bellou, whose kind attention and elegant hospitality, during the time I remained at Mortagne, I must ever remember with sentiments of sincere gratitude. This lady had invited Monsieur Lamorelie, the Sub-Prefect, one of the most elegant men I had met with in France, with several other gentlemen and ladies, to meet me. Among the party were Madame de Fontenay, Monsieur and Mademoiselle Claire de Vanssay--very agreeable people: the latter possessed, without great beauty, all the charms and vivacity of her country-women. In the evening we went to an assembly, where I had an opportunity of seeing, and being presented to, all the respectable families that yet remained in town; for at this season many were at their country-seats. The ease, elegance, and good manners of the company composing this society, I never saw excelled in any country. It is but common justice to observe, that in Mortagne, which is the residence of all the best families in the province, there is to be found all the characteristic good breeding for which the French were so long, and so deservedly celebrated.

The town of Mortagne stands on the declivity of a hill, in the province of Le Perche, bordering on Normandy. The high road to Bretagne passes through it. It has only one church remaining out of seven, six having been destroyed at the Revolution. It has some manufactories for serges and coarse cloths, and contains between five and six thousand inhabitants, in the department of L'Orne. From its elevated position and chalky soil, the air is pure and the situation healthy. The inhabitants are under the necessity of supplying themselves with water from the valley, as there are no wells on account of the rocky height it stands on, which is attended with inconvenience and expense; otherwise it would be a desirable residence for those who wish to unite economy with a change of climate.

During the Vendean war, this town became, at different periods, the victim of either party as they were successful; and it suffered severely. The hotel kept by Gautier (Les trois Lions), which is likewise la Poste, and le Bureau des Diligences, is the best, and the people are very obliging; but it partakes of the same want of cleanliness, that so invariably distinguishes all similar establishments in this country.

CHAP. III.

FROM MORTAGNE TO RENNES, SOEURS DE LA CHARITE. ALENCON, LAVAL, VITRE, THE RESIDENCE OF THE CELEBRATED MADAME DE SEVIGNE. RENNES.

I travelled by the diligence from Mortagne to Alencon and Laval: we arrived at the former place to dinner, and at the latter to remain all night. The carriage was filled with *Soeurs de la Charite*,

"Qui, pour le malheur seul connoissant la tendresse,
Aux besoins du vieil-age immollent leur jeunesse,"

on their way to different places in Bretagne, on charitable missions, by the order of the Superior at Paris. Four of these were young and beautiful women, none of whom could have attained the age of twenty; yet these females had already devoted themselves to attend on the sick and poor wherever their services might be required, for which purpose they receive a suitable education, in an Hospital at Paris, in such branches of medicine and surgery as may render them useful. They are distributed throughout the kingdom to attend the hospitals and prisons, which they do with the delicacy and attention peculiar to their sex. Of all the classes of females who thus devote themselves to a religious life, and to acts of charity, none are more respected, or more truly serviceable to their fellow-creatures. Their dress consists of a coarse brown jacket and gown, with a high linen cap, sloping down over the shoulders, and a rosary hanging round their waist.

Quitting Beauregard we crossed the river Sart: here the Province of Le Perche terminates, and we enter that of Normandy. For many miles, travelling close to the Forest of Bourse, the roads are excellent, though hilly, and the country highly cultivated in all directions. The peasantry were getting in the hay and rye harvest, and large tracts of wheat and barley were nearly ready for cutting.

The town of Alencon is the capital of L'Orne-sur-Sart. It stands in the middle of a fertile plain. The lace made here is the most valuable of any manufactured in France. The Hotel of the Prefecture is a fine building. After dinner I went to the theatre, (formerly an old manufactory), to see the **Hotel Garni** and **Les deux Suisses**: both performances were of a very moderate cast. The audience consisted principally of the military in garrison.

On the road from Alencon to Laval, we were guarded the whole day by two troopers of the Gendarmerie, who are quartered along the whole line of road from the capital; they are well armed and mounted, and keep a very vigilant guard. At every place we stopped our passports were examined. The police of this country is observed with greater rigor than at any former period of its history, with regard to passports. The circumstances under which the restoration took place, the political state of France, in regard to other powers, the conflicting interests and opinions of various parties, probably render it highly expedient. On the arrival of a stranger at Paris, his passport must be presented, and inscribed in the police book. The revision of the one under which the person has travelled is indispensably necessary. It is then carried to the British Ambassador, (if the stranger be of that nation), or to the minister of that country to which he belongs, where it must obtain the Ambassador's signature. It is next taken to the office of the Minister of Foreign Affairs, where it is deposited until the following day, for which ten livres are charged, and afterwards to the Prefecture of the Police, to be signed there in its turn: and when all this is done no one can quit the capital for the interior without its being again signed at the Prefecture of the police.

From Alencon, we passed the Briante, a small river, at Ville Neuve, where the road begins to skirt the Forest of Moultonue. At Mayenne, the river of that name divides the provinces. The whole of this country is singularly beautiful. I observed vast quantities of buck wheat, which the French call **bled noir** or **sarazin**. The country was very much enclosed, producing a great contrast to the vast tracts of land through which I had passed without a single division.

At two leagues from Mayenne we crossed the river Aisne, winding through a beautiful valley, between Martigne and Louverne. On the left the river forms a small lake, surrounded by a wood at the foot of a very long and steep hill.

The town of Mayenne is ancient and irregularly built, the river Mayenne running through it. The ruins of an old wall and some decayed towers remain of the fortifications which were taken by assault, after several bloody attempts, during the siege by the English, in 1424.

At Laval, where I stopped, after again crossing the Mayenne, I entered the province of Bretagne: it is an old dirty town, completely intersected by the river, and has a manufactory for coarse cloths and cottons. The **Tete Noire** is one of the worst inns I have met with in the country. The department of the Isle-et-Vilaine commences here.

This place is celebrated in the history of the Vendean war by the refuge Madame de Laroche-Jaquelin sought there, after the deplorable defeat of the royalist army at the battle of Mans, where it received its death-blow. The wreck of that army, under M. de Laroche-Jaquelin, were driven from it again on the following day, and from that hour never rallied so as to make any stand against the victorious republicans.

Quitting Laval the day after my arrival, I ascended a long and steep hill, travelled by the side of the forest of Petre, and came to Vitre, where I remained all night for the purpose of visiting the chateau of the celebrated Madame de Sevigne,[4] whose estate has descended to a distant branch of her family, who had the good fortune to save it from destruction during the revolution. The grounds are kept in excellent order. Her picture hangs in the apartment in which she composed her interesting and elegant letters, and every article of furniture carefully preserved is shown to strangers. The distance from Vitre to Rennes is seven leagues, over a road which becomes gradually less and less Interesting.

Rennes is the chief city of the Isle-et-Vilaine, and in former times was the capital of Bretagne. It is a large ancient built town, standing on a vast plain, between the rivers Isle and Vilaine. It has a hall of justice, (Cour Royale,) an episcopal palace,

---

4   Marie de Rabutin, Marchioness de Sevigne, was the daughter of the Baron de Chantal, and born in 1626: she espoused at the age of eighteen the Marquis de Sevigne, who fell in a duel in 1651, leaving her with one son and a daughter, to whose education she paid strict attention: the daughter married in 1669 the Count de Grignan, Commandant in Provence, and it was on a visit to her that the Marchioness caught a fever and died in 1696. Her son Charles, Marquis de Sevigne, was one of the admirers of Ninon de L'Enclos, and had a dispute with Madame Dacier respecting the sense of a passage in Horace. He died in 1713. (Moreri.)

and a foundry for cannon. A more dismal dirty looking city, or a more uninteresting one to a stranger, is seldom to be seen. Few traces remain of its ancient splendor; the old rampart, which once encompassed it, now forms a promenade.

Its commerce is considerable, being the entrepot for grain and cattle, with which it supplies Paris and the Southern Provinces, not so abundant in their produce. Jane of Flanders, Countess of Montfort, the most extraordinary woman of her time, resided here, during the imprisonment of her husband in the palace of the Louvre, by Philippe de Valois,[5] when Edward the Third of England invaded France. Hennebon, when attacked by Charles of Blois, was defended by the Countess, and relieved by Sir Walter Manny, whom Edward had sent with a body of 6,000 archers to her succour. The garrison, encouraged by so rare an example of female valour, defended themselves against an immense army, composed of French, Spaniards, Genoese, and Bretons, who frequently assaulted it, and were as vigorously repulsed. On one occasion, Froissart mentions her sallying out at the head of a body of two hundred cavalry, throwing the enemy into great confusion, doing great execution among them, and setting fire to the tents and magazines, which were entirely destroyed.

The population of Rennes is 27,000. It is at present garrisoned by one thousand troops, and people are of opinion that government finds it no easy task to keep down the spirit of the Vendeans, who are said to be, "plus Royalistes que le Roi". There appears every where a strong spirit of dissatisfaction on the part of the Royalists, at the general preference given to those who were employed under the late ruler in places of public trust, and who were avowed enemies to the restoration of Louis XVIII.

---

5   Among the brave knights who engaged in so many battles and perilous adventures, and other feats of arms, Froissart mentions Philip, as opposed to those heroes of high renown, Edward of England, the Prince of Wales his son, the Duke of Lancaster, Sir Reginald Lord Cobham, Sir Walter Manny of Hainault, Sir John Chandos, Sir Fulk Harley, and many others recorded in his book for worth and prowess. "In France also was found good chivalry, strong of limb and stout of heart, and in great abundance, for the kingdom of France was never brought so low as to want men ever ready for combat. Such was King Philipe de Valois, a bold and hardy knight, and his son King John, also John king of Bohemia, and Charles Count of Alencon his son".

CHAP. IV.

ROUTE FROM RENNES TO NANTES. CITY OF NANTES. HISTORICAL ANECDOTES.

Arriving at the first post, we crossed the river Vilaine, and between this and Rondun passed the river Bruck, and ascended a high mountain between Rondun and La Breharaye. At this place we quitted the department of the Isle-et-Vilaine. Crossing the Cher, we arrived at Derval, and from thence at Nozai, passing several large lakes, and then over the river Don. The whole of this distance, with the exception of the hill already mentioned, is composed of flat sandy plains, mostly uncultivated, and the road is very rough.

From Nozai to Ancenis we crossed the river Isac; from thence to Redon, Herie, to La Croix Blanche, along the bank of the river; and after mounting another steep hill, we descended into an extensive plain, leading to Gesvres and Nantes.

The whole of this country north of the Loire, from Rennes to Nantes, the triangular point resting upon Angers, is the country of the Chouans, which it is necessary, in reference to the Vendean war, to distinguish from the country south of the Loire, in the department of the Loire Inferieure, called le Bocage, or la Vendee. Although the latter was the scene of the more desperate warfare between the republicans and the royalists, yet the former had its share of bloodshed and misery. The whole country on both banks of the Loire, as far as Angers, is classic ground to those who revere the efforts by which the Vendeans so long resisted the republicans.

The city of Nantes is the chief seat of the Prefecture of the department of the Loire Inferieure, standing on the right bank of the river, surrounded by its ancient rampart, of a circular form, and in good preservation: on the opposite bank stand the ruined tower and mouldering bastions of Permil. This spot is interesting to an

Englishman, from the memorable events to which the fatal pretensions of Edward the Third gave rise, and which occupy the pages of French and English history, during a period of more than a century.[6]

---

6   In 1343, Edward the Third laid siege to this place. Froissart mentions the English army being drawn out on a hill, in battle array, near the town. The ground rises a little in this direction, but, I should suppose, it must have been on the right bank, as the country there is hilly, and this ancient fortress must have defended the passage of the river. "The king himself," says the Chronicle, "with the rest of his army, advanced towards Rennes, burning and ruining the country on all sides, and was most joyfully received by the whole army who lay before it, and had been there for a considerable time. When he had tarried there five days, he learned that the Lord Charles of Blois was at Nantes, collecting a large force of men at arms. He set out, therefore, leaving those whom he had found at Rennes, and came before Nantes, which he besieged as closely as he could, but was unable to surround it, such was its size and extent. The marshals, therefore, and their people, overran the country and destroyed it. The king of England, one day, drew out his army in battle array on a hill near Nantes, in expectation that the Lord Charles would come forth and offer him an opportunity of fighting with him: but, having waited from morning until noon in vain, they returned to their quarters: the light horse, however, in their retreat, galloped up to the barriers, and set fire to the suburbs".

"The king of England, during the siege, made frequent skirmishes, but without success, always losing some of his men; when, therefore, he found he could gain nothing by his assaults, and that the Lord Charles would not come out into the plains to fight him, he established there the Earl of Oxford, Sir Henry Beaumont, the Lord Percy, the Lord Roos, the Lord Mowbray, the Lord Delawar, Sir Reginald Cobham, Sir John Lisle, with six hundred men armed, and two hundred archers".

The king himself advanced into the country of Bretagne, wasting it wherever he went, until he came to the town of Dinant, of which Sir Peter Porteboeuf was governor. He immediately laid siege to it all round, and ordered it to be vigorously assaulted. Those within made a valiant resistance. Thus did the king of England in one season, and in one day, make an assault by himself, or those ordered by him, upon three cities in Bretagne, and a good town, viz. Rennes, Vannes, and Nantes. The brave Sir Walter Manny was left before Vannes, with five hundred men at arms, and six thousand archers, while the king with the rest of his army advanced towards Rennes and Nantes. This gallant soldier, at the battle of Calais, had this singular honour conferred on him by his sovereign, who, with his valiant son the Prince of Wales, both served under his banner.--Edward said to Sir Walter Manny, "Sir Walter, I will that you be the chief of this enterprise, and I and my son will fight under your banner".

The lively and picturesque historian then gives a very interesting account of the above action, which was fought the last day of December 1348, and of the gallantry of Edward's conduct to his prisoner, Sir Eustace de Ribeaumont.

"We will now speak of the King of England, who was there incognito, under Sir Walter Manny's banner. He advanced with his men on foot, to meet the enemy, who were formed in close order, with their pikes shortened to five feet, planted out before them. The first attack was very sharp and severe. The King singled out Sir Eustace de Ribeaumont, who was a strong and hardy knight: he fought a long time marvellously well with the King, so that it was a pleasure to see them; but, by the confusion of the engagement, they were separated; for two large bodies met where they were fighting, and forced them to break off the combat.

"On the side of the French there was excellent fighting, by Sir Geoffrey de Chargny, Sir John de Landas, Sir Hector, and Sir Gavin de Ballieul, and others; but they were all surpassed by Sir Eustace de Ribeaumont, who that day struck the King twice down on his knees: at last, however, he was obliged to present his sword to the King, saying, 'Sir Knight, I surrender myself your prisoner, for the honour of the day must fall to the English.'

"All that belonged to Sir Geoffry de Chargny were either slain or captured: among the first was Sir Henry du Bois, and Sir Peppin de Werre; Sir Geoffry and the rest were taken prisoners. The last that was taken, and who in that day had excelled all, was Sir Eustace de Ribeaumont.

"When the engagement was over, the King returned to the Castle at Calais, and ordered all the prisoners to be brought before him. The French taken, knew for the first time, that the King of England had been there in person, under the banner of Sir Walter de Manny.

"The King said he would this evening of the new year entertain them all at supper in the Castle. When the hour for supper was come, the tables spread, and the King and his Knights dressed in new robes, as well as the French, who, notwithstanding they were prisoners, made good cheer (for the King wished it should be so), the King seated himself at table, and made those Knights do the same around him in a most honourable manner. The gallant Prince of Wales, and the Knights of England, served up the first course, and waited on their guests. At the second course, they went and seated themselves at another table, where they were served, and attended on very quietly.

"When supper was over, and the tables removed, the King remained in the Hall among the English and French Knights, bare-headed, except a chaplet of fine pearls, which was round his head. He conversed with all of them; but when he came to Sir Geoffry de Chargny, his countenance altered, and looking at him askance, he said, 'Sir Geoffry, I have but little reason to love you, when you wished to seize upon me by stealth last night, what had given me so much trouble to acquire, and cost me such sums of money' (Sir Geoffry had endeavoured to bribe the garrison to put him in possession of it in the night previous to the battle): 'I am, however, rejoiced to have caught you thus in attempting it.'--When he came to Sir Eustace de Ribeaumont, he assumed a cheerful look, and said with a smile, 'Sir Eustace, you are the most valiant knight in Christendom that I ever saw attack his enemy, or defend himself. I never yet found any one in battle, who, body to body, had given me so much to do as you have done this day. I adjudge to you the prize of valour, above all the knights of my Court, as what is justly due to you.'--The King then took off his chaplet, which was very rich and handsome, and placing it on the head of Sir Eustace, said, 'Sir Eustace, I present you with this chaplet, as being the best combatant this day, either within or without doors; and I beg of you to wear it this year for the love of me. I know that you are lively and amorous, and love the company of ladies and damsels; therefore say, wherever you go, that I gave it to you. I also give you your liberty, free of ransom; and you may set out to-morrow, and go whither you will.'"]

The river Loire, which is crossed by seven bridges, winds through the town. They are the Pont Rousseau, De Permil, D'Aiguillon, Feydeau, De la Belle Croix, Brisebois, and Toussaint. The houses are regular and handsome, having in some places a very singular appearance, from the ground having sunk, and the foundations given way, causing them to lean in various directions from the perpendicular line. In point of commerce, at one period antecedent to the Revolution, Nantes was the most considerable sea-port in France: since the loss of its West India trade, especially with Saint Domingo, it has been greatly reduced. The rich plains which surround it on three sides, in the form of an amphitheatre, and the river covered with vessels and boats, give it a most lively appearance. It has a large Theatre, a Royal College (lately the Lyceum), a Commercial Tribunal, a handsome Exchange, a Bishop's Palace, Hall of the Prefecture, Public Library, Anatomical and Surgical Academies, Botanical Garden, Museum of Natural History, and a foundry for cannon.

The latter is in the old and decaying Chateau on the bank of the river, called Goulemme. One of its bastions was blown up a few years since by accident, which has shaken and destroyed the whole fabric; but it is still capable of holding a garrison, and is a fine monument of ancient fortification. It was once the residence of Henry IV. of France, at the time he signed the celebrated edict, (1598,) in favour of the reformed religion, afterwards revoked by Louis XIV. in 1685, and which occasioned such deplorable consequences to the French nation.

M. de Sainte Foix, in his historical Essays upon Paris, vol. i. p. 113, speaking of the Rue de Grenelle, in the quarter of Saint Eustache, gives the following curious account of the birth of this great King, whose memory is revered in France, beyond that of all the other monarchs who have swayed the Gallic sceptre.

"Jeanne d'Albret, being desirous of following her husband to the wars of Picardy, the King her father told her, that in case she proved with child, he wanted her to come and lie-in at his house; and that he would bring up the child himself, whether a boy or a girl. This Princess finding herself pregnant, and in her ninth month, set out from Compiegne, passed through all France as far as the Pyrenees, and arrived in fifteen days at Pau in Bearn. She was very desirous to see her father's will. It was contained in a thick gold box, on which was a gold chain, that would have gone twenty-five or thirty times round her neck. She asked it of him:--'It shall be yours,' said he, 'as soon as you have shown me the child that you now carry; and that you may not bring into the world a crying or a pouting child, I promise you the whole, provided that whilst you are in labour, you sing the Bearnese song ***Notre Dame du bout du Pont aidez-moi en cette heure***". No sooner was the Princess safely delivered, than her father, placing the gold chain on her neck, and giving her the gold box wherein was his will, said to her: 'These are for you, daughter, but this is for me;' and took the child in his gown, without waiting for its being dressed in form, and carried it into his chamber. The little Prince was brought up in such a manner as to be able to undergo fatigue and hardship; frequently eating nothing but common bread. The good King his grandfather ordered it thus, and would not let him be delicately pampered, in order that from his infancy he might be inured to privation. He has often been seen, according to the custom of the country, amongst the other children of the Castle and village of Coirazze, bare-footed and bare-headed, as well in winter as in summer. Who was this Prince?--Henry IV.

"Being descended from the Kings of France, he became the heir to that Kingdom; but as he was educated a Protestant, his claim was resisted. He early distinguished himself by feats of arms. After the peace of Saint Germain, in 1570, he was taken to the French Court, and two years afterwards married Margaret, sister of Charles IX. (At the rejoicings on this occasion the infamous massacre of ***La Saint Barthelemy*** took place.) In 1589 he succeeded to the throne of France; but his religion proving an obstacle to his coronation, he consented to abjure it in 1593. In 1598 he issued the edict of Nantes, granting toleration to the Protestants".

Mezeray, speaking of the marriage of the King of Navarre (afterwards Henry IV.) with Margaret de Valois, says, "There were many diversions, tournaments, and ballets at Court; and amongst others, one which seemed to presage the calamity that was so near bursting out upon the Huguenots--the King and his brothers defending Paradise against the King of Navarre and his brothers, who were repulsed and banished to Hell;" and Sainte Foix, in his relation of the horrible massacre, gives a detail, which in the present age appears almost incredible.

Catherine of Medicis, whose abominable politics had corrupted the disposition of her son, was at the head of the cabinet council who agreed to the murder of more than one hundred thousand Protestants; and the miserable bigot Charles IX. stationed during the massacre at the window of a house then belonging to the

Constable of Bourbon, fired with his own hands upon the Huguenots with a long blunderbuss, whilst they were trying to escape across the river.

The River Erdre runs northward of the city, and forms a beautiful feature, winding for many miles among cultivated fields and woodlands, through a country agreeably diversified with villas, to which the wealthier inhabitants retire during the summer months. The river resembles a lake for the greater part of its course, and is called the Barban.

The Gothic church of Saint Pierre, built by the English in 1434, is a fine old structure: having been much neglected for many years, and greatly defaced during the Revolution, it was at this time restoring. Among the monuments about to be replaced, was an excellent one of Anne de Bretagne, whose effigy, and that of her husband, are as large as life. The allegorical figures of Justice, Temperance, Prudence, and Fortitude, the twelve Apostles, and the supporters to the Arms (a greyhound and a lion), are all executed in the finest white marble. They were hidden during the Revolution, and have only very lately been discovered, as have also some capital paintings piously preserved for the Church. Anne was first married to Charles VIII. in 1499, and afterwards to Louis XII. She died at the Chateau de Blois in 1514, and Louis in 1515.

The climate of Nantes is mild, and reckoned remarkably healthy: every article of life is cheap, and from its mild temperature it abounds in the finest fruits and most excellent wines. Its population is estimated at 60,000 inhabitants. The numbers that were destroyed during the Revolution, or, as the French emphatically term it, "Le regne de la Terreur," were never ascertained; but the frightful history of that bloody period would probably justify the computation at half the number of its present population, many having fallen victims to the murders that were termed "*Noyades*," independent of those who perished in the Vendean war.

The spot where the gallant Charette was shot, with several other leaders of the Vendean army, is shown; and in the cemetery, a large mound of earth marks the place where the bodies were thrown in, at the time of the "*Fuzillades*" when the infamous Carrier presided at the execution of the brave Royalists.[7] The print

7   Chaque nuit on venait en prendre par centaines, pour les mettre sur les bateaux. La on liait les malheureux deux a deux, et on les poussait dans l'eau a coups de baionette. On saisissait indistinctement tout ce qui se trouvait a l'entrepot, tellement qu'on noya un jour l'etat major d'une corvette Anglaise, qui etait prisonnier de guerre. Une autre fois, Carrier, voulant donner un exemple de

beneath represents this monster on the banks of the Loire directing the Noyades.

At the end of a fine avenue of trees, on the Boulevard, is a large and splendid mansion built by that Deputy, and which is at present inhabited by a merchant. Carrier's mistress (to whom he left it, together with a very considerable fortune, amassed from the spoils of his plunder, and the murder of the innocent inhabitants) was very lately sentenced to two years' hard labour for some crime she had committed: and it is no less remarkable, that, of the remaining inhabitants known to have participated in the atrocities of that frightful period, there is not one but is reduced to poverty, and most of them in the extreme of wretchedness, shunned by all, and suffering the ignominy they have so justly merited!

l'austerite des moeurs republicaines, fit enfermer trois cent filles publiques de la ville, et les malheureuses creatures furent noyees. Enfin, l'on estime qu'il a peri a l'entrepot quinze mille personnes en un mois.--*Memoires de Madame la Marquise de Laroche-Jaquelin.*

CHAP. V.

COUNTRY SOUTH OF THE LOIRE.--LE BOCAGE.--CLISSON.--HIS-
TORICAL ANECDOTES.--THE GARENNE, AND RIVER SEVRES.

The best method of travelling in this country is on horseback: in fact, it is impossible to proceed in any other way, after quitting the main road. Having procured a guide and horses, I set out early in the morning, crossing the Loire by the Pont Rosseau, to Verton, keeping along the banks of the River Sevres. Verton is a romantic village standing on a hill: most of the houses are in ruins, from the effect of the destructive war of La Vendee. From thence to Le Palet, most intricate narrow roads, or more properly speaking, pathways, darkened by the overhanging branches of trees, and in many parts deep with mire, from the sun's rays not being able to dry the ground, make it difficult to proceed, and we several times lost our way. It was late before we reached Le Palet, and though I had not tasted food for many hours, I could not resist stopping to view so interesting a spot, and making a hasty sketch of the ruins of the house in which Abelard was born, and in which Heloise resided with him before their final separation. The ruins of the House of Berenger, the father of Abelard, are close to the church of Palet, on the left of the high road, three miles distant from Clisson. Le Palet is thus described by a French author, in the history of the Province.

"Cet homme si celebre par son savoir, ses amours, et ses infortunes, amena Heloise au Palet lorsqu'il l'eut enlevee de chez le Chanoine Fulbert, pour la soustraire au ressentiment de cet oncle jaloux et barbare; mais, oblige de quitter cette retraite paisible pour retourner a Paris, ou l'appelaient ses nombreux disciples, le soin de sa gloire et de sa fortune, Abelard confia a sa soeur sa chere Heloise et le gage precieux qu'elle portait dans son sein. Elle accoucha au Palet d'un fils d'une si rare beaute, qu'elle le nomma Astralabe, c'est-a-dire, astre brillant; mais l'absence de celui qu'elle adorait rendait moins vifs pour elle les doux plaisirs de la maternite; son ame expansive et brulante etait livree sans cesse a une inquiete et sombre melancholie qu'elle ne parvenait sans doute a dissiper qu'en venant sur les bords de la Sevres rever a l'objet de sa tendresse, et soupirer apres son retour. Sept siecles se sont ecoules depuis cette epoque, et les noms d'Abelard et d'Heloise embellissent toujours ce delicieux ravage. On interroge avec une curiosite avide ces roches eternelles et ces grottes mysterieuses qui furent les temoins discrets de leurs peines et de leurs plaisirs. On se reporte a ces temps recules ou ces amants venaient dans cette solitude enchanteresse, se confier mutuellement leur vifs inquietudes; on croit les voir s'egarer sous ces riants ombrages, et s'abandonner a toutes les inspirations de l'eloquence, a toutes les illusions de l'amour".

I arrived at Clisson just as the sun was disappearing, and its rays were only sufficiently strong to reflect the ruined towers of the Castle in the river which runs at its foot. It will be much easier to imagine, than for me to convey the sensations I felt when I first caught a glimpse of it, with the story of La Roche-Jaquelin full in my recollection! I alighted at a small cabaret, dignified by the appellation of the Hotel de la Providence, which seemed preferable to another recommended to me by my guide,--such an one, indeed, as might be expected in a remote place like this: part of the roof was off, and, like most of the houses in the place, bore evident marks of the desolating war that had been carried on here: many are still in ruins. The descent into the town is very steep and rugged, the road being formed out of the solid rock. The master of the cabaret was sitting with his family at the door, but the appearance of his mansion was so unpromising, that I thought it best to make some agreement, and a few inquiries before dismounting;--these preliminaries being settled, and having consented to pay him fifty sous for supper and my bed, and thirty for breakfast, I entered the house: and never recollect having a keener relish for a meal, or enjoying one more heartily, for I had been sixteen hours on horseback.

Fatigued and exhausted as I was, I rambled after dinner towards the delightful grounds of La Garenne, belonging to Monsieur La Motte, who has embellished them in a most interesting and romantic manner.

The river Sevres runs along the side, and separates them from the fine old Castle of Clisson, whose high and decaying towers and battlements give the beholder a noble idea of its ancient grandeur. The evening was a very fine one,--one of those delightful soft, clear skies usual at this season, the latter end of July. I sat myself down in the grotto of Heloise,--a spot of the deepest seclusion, formed, by the hand of Nature, of large masses of granite. The nightingales were singing in the lofty trees at the back; on the sides were shrubs of every description intermingled with fruit trees, and the river having several falls and little rocky islets, gave an air of delightful enchantment to this most romantic scene.

Heloise! a ce nom, qui ne doit s'attendrir?
Comme elle sut aimer! comme elle sut souffrir!

At the entrance of the grotto are engraved these lines, nearly effaced by the hand of time.

Heloise peut-etre erra sur ce rivage,
Quand, aux yeux des jaloux derobant son sejour,
Dans les murs du Palet elle vint mettre au jour
Un fils, cher et malheureux gage
De ses plaisirs furtifs et de son tendre amour.
Peut-etre en ce reduit sauvage,
Seule, plus d'une fois, elle vint soupirer,
Et gouter librement la douceur de pleurer;
Peut-etre sur ce roc assise
Elle revait a son malheur.
J'y veux rever aussi; j'y veux remplir mon coeur
Du doux souvenir d'Heloise.

I had but a few weeks before seen the tomb of Abelard and Heloise in the Cemetery of Pere la Chaise at Paris, whither it had been recently removed from the Convent of the Augustins, at which latter place I had formerly made the annexed drawing of it. I had likewise been very lately at Argenteuil, once the place of her asylum described by Pope:

    In these deep solitudes and awful cells--

and had the same day witnessed the ruins of the house in which Abelard was born, and in which Heloise resided and became a mother, and from whence she used to make frequent visits to this spot: all these circumstances combined, gave the scene before me a most powerful interest. I rose early the next day, anxious to revisit a place which had afforded me such delight the previous evening. Wandering by the beautiful banks of the river, along its green meadows, in a woody recess, I observed the following lines beneath an urn, cut in the rock on which it rested:

Consacrer dans l'obscurite,
Ses loisirs a l'etude, a l'amitie sa vie,
Sont des plaisirs dignes d'envie;
Etre cheri vaut mieux qu'etre vante!

A little further on, is a stone pillar, with a venerable accacia tree spreading its leaves over it. It has the following Latin inscription:

VII

IM CAESAR
AVGVSTVS
PONTIFEX MAX
VIAM. OLIM
A CONIVINCO
AD LIMONEM

IMP. CAESAR. TRAJ.
ADRIANVS AVG
PM. TRIB. POT.
VIAM AB AVGVSTO
STATAM REFICIT.[8]

8   Auguste etendit jusqu'a La Loire La Gaule Aquitanique, autrefois bornee par la Garonne, et comprit L'Armorique dans la Province Celtique ou Lyonnaise. L'Empereur Adrian, ayant fait depuis une nouvelle distribution des Gaules, divisa La Lyonnaise en deux, et mit L'Armorique dans la seconde; enfin cette Lyonnaise ou Celtique ayant ete encore divisee en deux, Tours devint la Metropole de la

Farther on several large blocks of granite are piled together in so strange and curious a manner, that it must have been the work of Nature alone:--one of them has these beautiful lines carved on it:

O! Limpide Riviere! O Riviere cherie!
Puisse la sotte vanite
Ne jamais dedaigner ta rive humble et fleurie!
Que ton simple sentier ne soit point frequente
Par aucun tourment de la vie
Tels que l'ambition, l'envie,
L'avarice, et la faussete!
Un bocage si frais, un sejour si tranquille,
Aux tendres sentiments doit seul servir d'azile.
Ces rameaux amoureux entrelasses expres
Aux Muses, aux Amours, offrent leur voile epais;
Et ce cristal d'une onde pure
A jamais ne doit reflechir
Que les graces de la nature
Et les images du plaisir.

Close to the brink of the river stands a prodigiously large granite rock, immediately facing the waterfall called le Bassin de Diane: on it are these words:

SA MASSE INDESTRVCTIBLE
A FATIGVE LE TEMS.
a quotation from Delille.

The French writers, speaking of this interesting place, observe: "Comment soupconner en effet qu'au milieu de cette *terrible Vendee*, qu'au centre de cet impenetrable et sombre Bocage, il existe un pays delicieux et fertile, couvert de mines seculaires qui rappelent tous les souvenirs historiques de notre ancienne France, comme le caractere de ses habitans en rappele les moeurs, le courage, et la loyaute".

---

troisieme, qui comprenait la Touraine, le Maine, l'Anjou, et la Bretagne.--*Histoire de Bret*.

On the opposite side of the river, a little to the right, stands the ancient Chateau de Clisson, celebrated in the modern as well as the ancient history of Bretagne. Its lofty turrets, and decaying bastions, extend a considerable distance along the shore of the Sevres, recalling to mind the ancient days of chivalry, when bravery, love, and religion, were so singularly blended together, and gave a romantic half-polished manner to the greatest barbarians. In later times it became the scene of events which no one can contemplate without the deepest interest. In viewing this magnificent ruin, it is impossible not to regret that a place so frequently the theatre of noble achievements, inhabited by one of the greatest men that France has produced, Francois I. Connetable de Clisson,[9] father to Anne of Bretagne, should have been so recently the scene of such savage horrors and bloodshed! Now, all is silence and solitude: and amidst the noble ruins which were once decorated with banners, and the hard-earned trophies of victory,--where high-born knights and splendid dames mingled in mirth and festivity to the echoes of the minstrels, singing lays of love or battle,--are now only to be seen and heard the birds of prey, hovering over a solitary tree, planted to mark the spot where a deed was committed which has not often its parallel in the darkest histories of the most ferocious nations.

---

9   In the "Histoire Genealogique de France", tom. vi. is an account of the Constable's death. "The Duke of Orleans, brother to the king, was very fond of a Jewess, whom he privately visited. Having some reason to suspect that Peter de Craon, Lord of Sable and de la Ferte-Bernard, his chamberlain and favourite, had joked with the Duchess of Orleans upon his intrigue, he turned him out of his house with infamy. Craon imputed his disgrace partly to the Constable of Clisson. On the night of the 13th June, having waited for him at the corner of the street *Coulture Ste. Catherine*, and finding he had but little company with him, he fell upon him at the head of a score of ruffians. Clisson defended himself for some time without any other weapon than a small cutlass; but after receiving three wounds, fell from his horse, and pitched against a door, which flew open. The report of this assassination reached the king's ears just as he was stepping into bed. He put on a great coat and his shoes, and repaired to the place where he was informed his constable had been killed. He found him in a baker's shop, wallowing in his blood. After his wounds were examined, "Constable, (said he to him), nothing was or ever will he so severely punished". It was given out that Clisson made his will the next day, and there was a mighty outcry about the sum of 1,700,000 livres, which it amounted to. It should be observed, that during twenty-five years that he was in the service of France, he had sought for and beaten the English every where; that he gained the famous battle of Robeck, and chastised the Flemish; that he enjoyed for twelve years the salary and appointments of Constable; and that, moreover, his landed estate, (which included many castles inherited from his ancestors, in Bretagne and Poitou,) was very considerable."

During the Vendean war, the royalists had been driven out of Clisson by the republicans, under the command of a ferocious jacobin. The town was pillaged and burnt before they quitted it. Twenty-seven females had, during the battle, concealed themselves among the ruins: when information of it was given to the troops, who had already quitted the place, they were ordered to return, and the whole of these unhappy women were thrown alive into a well, where they perished!!! It has since been filled up, and the lonely tree, just mentioned, now records the bloody and inhuman deed.

In the account of Clisson, by a late French author, no notice is taken of this circumstance. He merely observes, when mentioning the destruction of the place, after the de la Roche-Jaquelin had quitted it, "Les Rives ombragees de la Sevres, si seduisante par ses belles cascades et l'ensemble de ce paysage poetique, feroient de cette contree un sejour delicieux, si de tristes debris, qui heureusement disparoissent tous les jours, ne rappelaient encore le souvenir affligeant de nos discordes civiles. Les armees Revolutionnaires qui combattirent les Vendeens, en 1793 et en 1794, employerent inutilement pour les reduire le fer et le feu; la flamme atteignit les villes, les villages, les metairies, et jusqu'aux humbles chaumieres; et, dans ce vaste et epouvantable incendie, Clisson ne put echapper a une ruine complete. Jamais peut-etre cette petite ville ne se seroit entierement reedifie, sans une circonstance particuliere qui contribua puissamment a la faire renoitre de ces cendres".

In the town of Clisson was born the celebrated Barin de la Galissonniere, Admiral of France, who fought the well-known action off Mahon, in the month of June, 1756, with Admiral Byng, who, in consequence of his conduct on that occasion, was brought to a court martial and shot. The French writers make the following absurd remark, as to the *cause* of his fate: "Les Anglais, furieux d'avoir ete vaincus par un Amiral Francois, firent fusiller l'Amiral Byng". It is now well known that he was sacrificed to an unprincipled ministerial faction.

The ancient Chateau de Clisson is built on a rock, on the bank of the Sevres, facing the mouth of the river, called Le Moine, which empties itself into the Sevres at this place, so that the town of Clisson stands between the two rivers at their junction. An ancient bridge, from whence this view is taken, joins one part of the town to the other, and leads to the castle, which was once considered the barrier of Bretagne. The two rivers run over a bed of granite rock, which, in some places, forming a cataract, adds considerably to the surrounding scenery: large masses of this rock in many parts seem as if piled up by nature for the purpose of giving it a more romantic effect. The whole forms a most picturesque object, when viewed from the opposite shore, from whence the sketch of the temple erected on the ruin of St. Gilles is taken; and the remembrance of its recent fate throws over the scene a strong and melancholy interest.

The castle is supposed to have been first erected by the Romans, as the Province formed a part of the Gaule Aquitanique, under the Emperors Augustus and Adrian.

The French repaired it during the reign of Louis VIII. in 1223, under Olivier I. Sire de Clisson, as he is styled; and it was made a regular fortification, and surrounded by a wall a century after, by the Connetable: in 1464 the Duc de Bretagne, Francis II. entirely finished it.

The Sire de Clisson, Olivier I. who had served during one of the Crusades in Palestine, was knighted with several others, in 1218. "Un nombre prodigieux de Seigneurs Anglais, Normands, Angevins, Manceaux, Tourangeaux, et Bretons, prirent la Croix; Le Pape, Innocent III. envoya en Bretagne, en 1197, Helvain, Moine de St. Denis, pour y precher une croisade. Une grande quantite de Bretons se laisserent conduire en Syrie par ce Moine; et, en 1218, plusieurs Seigneurs Bretons suivirent leur exemple, entre autres, Herve de Leon, Morvau, Vicomte du Fou, et le Sire de Clisson".

From the construction of the towers and bastions, it is supposed that at his return from the Holy Land, he had copied the Syrian style of building; and one of the towers, which is represented in the sketch of the gateway of the Chateau de Clisson, is still called La Tour des Pelerins.

This tower, which has been used as a dungeon, is the most perfect of any remaining. In it are subterranean galleries, anciently used as a prison, and appropriated by the republicans to the same purpose. It is dreadful to think of the horrors that have been practised within its walls, in our own time.

From the top of this tower the prospect is very extensive, and, during the year 1793, when the republican army quartered themselves in it, a sentinel was placed there to give notice in case of the approach of an enemy. The historian of that period, speaking of the entrance to this tower, observes, in reference to the cruelties committed there in the Vendean war:

"Il existait au milieu de la derniere cour un tres beau puits, taille dans le roc et extremement profond: il est actuellement comble, et ma plume se refuse a tracer les scenes horribles qui ensanglanterent ce lieu en 1793 et en 1795, tristes et epouvantables effets des guerres civiles!"

This passage alludes, I imagine, to the circumstance related in page 90. Within its walls are various inscriptions, many of them in characters so difficult to decypher, that they remain unknown. The following has been rendered into more modern French by Cerutti.

> J'ai gravi, mesure ces ruines sublimes;
> Mon coeur s'en est emu! De nos vaillants aieux
> Tout y representait les tournois magnanimes,
> Ils semblaient reparoitre et combattre a mes yeux;
> J'entendois sous leurs coups retentir les abimes;
> Juge de leurs combats, idole de leur coeur,
> Du haut des tours, la dame admiroit le vainqueur.
> Casques et boucliers, cuirasses gigantesques,
> Cris d'armes, mot d'amour, devises de l'honneur,
> Carlets pour l'infidele ou pour le suborneur,
> Tout garde sur ces murs vraiment chevaleresques.
> La memoire d'un siecle ou l'epee, ou la foi,
> Ou la galanterie etaient la seule loi.

Louis IX. and Blanche of Castille, his queen, retired to Clisson, at the time the English, under Henry III. penetrated into Poitou, and were received by Olivier de Clisson, who then garrisoned it.

In the war of the League, which convulsed the kingdom of France, Clisson remained faithful to Henry III. and during the early part of the reign of his successor Henry IV. The Protestants were there protected, and established themselves in the fauxbourg. From the period at which Henry IV. signed the edict at Nantes, 15th April, 1598, until the war of La Vendee, this celebrated fortress is no where mentioned by any of the French historians: it became neglected when the feudal system declined, and the republican army completed its ruin. The sad events of this period, and the destruction and carnage which followed, can never be effaced from the page of history. The ruined towns and villages prove the melancholy truth, that the general corruption of a nation prepares the way for general anarchy, and that the blindness of political rage is always more vindictive than even private hatred.

I can never sufficiently lament the absence, at this time, of Madame de La Roche-Jaquelin from the country, as she occasionally resides in the neighbourhood, since the restoration of her property, (although her once noble residence is now in a state of ruin,) occupying a small chateau at some small distance, which had partly escaped the fire and destruction that had been fatal to most houses in the district. Who can read the interesting memoirs of this Lady, and not sympathize in the sufferings of herself, and of those brave and loyal people whose heroic struggle against their republican oppressors lasted with little intermission from the overthrow of the monarchy until its final restoration? Among the number of heroic females who, like Madame de la Roche-Jaquelin, thus distinguished themselves, was Madame de La Rochefoucault who, like her admirer Charette, was put to death at Nantes. This lady, of an ancient and noble family, and of great beauty, signalized herself on various occasions, but being taken prisoner at the battle of the Moulin aux Chevres, she was immediately shot!

The whole history of this terrible war is filled with the noble devotion of heroic females. The chiefs were attended in the most sanguinary battles by ladies, who had themselves ornamented their standards with loyal and chivalrous emblems of the cause for which they were prepared to sacrifice themselves, and who were frequently seen rallying the broken troops, and falling, covered with wounds, by the hands of their enemies!

The annexed view of the Moulin aux Chevres, which is rendered interesting from the account given by Madame de la Roche-Jaquelin of the battle fought near it, will convey a tolerable idea of the scenery of the country.

The prodigious growth of the willow tree in Bretagne, is such as to claim the peculiar notice of travellers: here they attain a gigantic height, no where else to be seen. Batard, in his "***Notices sur les Vegetaux***" mentions one in the commune of Pommeraie in the arrondissement de Beaupreau, whose age was supposed to be nearly two thousand years. Within the Chateau at Clisson are some very old ones, but the finest I observed were at the Moulin aux Chevres.

CHAP. VI.

LIMITS AND GENERAL APPEARANCE OF LE BOCAGE. MODE OF
WARFARE PRACTISED BY THE VENDEANS.

My opportunity of becoming acquainted with that singular district called Le Bocage, will be best understood by very briefly sketching my route through it. I traversed it, and the district called Le Loroux, by the route of Montaigne and Lege, and on my return I passed through Clisson, Vallet, and Loroux, along the banks of the Loire. By pursuing this route, I had every where the interesting opportunity of exploring the scene of that destructive warfare which had ravaged the towns and villages of this part of France.

At one period, the war of La Vendee extended to the north of the Loire, as far as Rennes, forming a triangle, the eastern point of which rested on the town of Angers. To the south of the Loire it spread nearly as far as la Rochelle; and as in this part also it extended nearly to Angers, the tract over which it spread its ravages formed nearly a square. The district called Loroux runs parallel with the Loire: Le Bocage, which occupies both districts, and the whole country south of that river, is comprehended under the general appellation of La Vendee. Under the old divisions of France Le Bocage formed part of the province of Poitou, and Le Loroux part of the provinces of Anjou and Bretagne: but when, at the revolution, France was divided into departments, these two districts were denominated La Vendee, Les deux Sevres, La Loire Inferieure, and Mayenne and Loire.

La Vendee is an extremely interesting district, not merely on account of the singular and heroic warfare that was carried on there so long, but also from the appearance of the country, and the manners, opinions, and general character of its inhabitants; and Le Bocage is, in all these respects, the most interesting part of

La Vendee. In Le Bocage, the war was carried on with most wonderful vigour and pertinacity, as well as with almost unparalleled destruction and cruelty. Those who are acquainted only with the other parts of France, can form no idea of the aspect of this district, or of the manners of its inhabitants; they differ so widely and essentially, that they seem to belong to another portion of the globe. It has always been regarded as the most fertile country in France; and, before the revolution, it was undoubtedly one of the most populous.

There are only two roads in the whole country: one of them runs from Nantes to la Rochelle, and the other from Bordeaux to Tours, through Poitou: all the rest of this district is a complete labyrinth: there are indeed numerous pathways, so very winding and narrow, that they are much more calculated to harass and mislead, than to assist a traveller in his journey: these pathways are flanked by wide and deep ditches, and almost rendered completely dark by lofty hedges on each side of them, the trees of which meet at top, and thus form an arch: hence they are rough and uneven in summer, besides being intolerably hot, and deep and miry in winter. To add to these inconveniences, the bed of a rivulet flowing along them frequently constitutes the only passage. Even when the traveller, after toiling along these dreadful pathways, comes near a town or village, he generally finds that the approach to it is practicable only by ascending irregular steps, cut out of the solid rock, on which they are built. The inhabitants themselves even are frequently puzzled by these pathways; and, after wandering for a considerable length of time, at last find out that they have been travelling in a wrong direction.

The whole country bears the appearance of an extensive and thick forest: this arises from the nature of the enclosures; they are extremely small, often not more than fifty or sixty perches, surrounded with strong hedges planted in the banks. These circumstances alone would give the appearance just noticed; but the effect is much increased from other causes. On each side of the banks, on which the trees are planted, there are ditches and drains, and the moisture which they constantly supply to their roots, renders their growth very rapid and luxuriant; so that when we consider the number of the trees and their great size, we shall not be surprised that the country looks like an immense forest. Sometimes the trees are so disposed as to answer the purpose of a palisade; and this purpose they answer most effectually, not only from the great size and strength of the trees themselves, but also from the intervening spaces between them being filled up with strong and impassable underwood.[10]

10   A tract of about 150 miles square, at the mouth and on the southern bank of the Loire, comprehends the scene of those deplorable hostilities. The most inland part of the district, and that in which the insurrection first broke out, is called *Le Bocage*; and seems to have been almost as singular in its physical conformation, as in the state and condition of its population. A series of detached eminences, of no great elevation, rose over the whole face of the country, with little rills trickling in the hollows and occasional cliffs by their sides. The whole space was divided into small enclosures, each surrounded with tall wild hedges, and rows of pollard trees; so that though there were few large woods, the whole region had a sylvan and impenetrable appearance. The ground was mostly in pasturage; and the landscape had, for the most part, an aspect of wild verdure, except that in the autumn some patches of yellow corn appeared here and there athwart their green enclosures. Only two great roads traversed this sequestered region, running nearly parallel, at a distance of more than seventy miles from each other. In the intermediate space, there was nothing but a labyrinth of wild and devious paths, crossing each other at the extremity of almost every field--often serving, at the same time, as channels for the winter torrents, and winding so capriciously among the innumerable hillocks, and beneath the meeting hedge-rows, that the natives themselves were always in danger of losing their way when they went a league or two from their own habitations. The country, though rather thickly peopled, contained, as may be supposed, few large towns; and the inhabitants, devoted almost entirely to rural occupations, enjoyed a great deal of leisure. The noblesse or gentry of the country were very generally resident on their estates, where they lived in a style of simplicity and homeliness which had long disappeared from every other part of the kingdom. No grand parks, fine gardens, or ornamented villas; but spacious clumsy chateaux, surrounded with farm offices and cottages for the labourers. Their manners and way of life, too, partook of the same primitive rusticity. There was great cordiality, and even much familiarity, in the intercourse of the seigneurs with their dependants. They were followed by large trains of them in their hunting expeditions, which occupied so great a part of their time. Every man had his fowling-piece, and was a marksman of fame or pretensions. They were posted in various quarters, to intercept or drive back the game; and were thus trained, by anticipation, to that sort of discipline and concert, in which their whole art of war was afterwards found to consist. Nor was their intimacy confined to their sports. The peasants resorted familiarly to their landlords for advice, both legal and medical; and they repaid the visits in their daily rambles, and entered with interest into all the details of their agricultural operations. They came to the weddings of their children, drank with their guests, and made little presents to the young people. On Sundays and holidays, all the retainers of the family assembled at the chateau, and danced in the barn or the court-yard, according to the season. The ladies of the house joined in the festivity, and that without any airs of condescension or of mockery; for, in their own life, there was little splendour or luxurious refinement. They travelled on horseback, or in heavy carriages drawn by oxen; and had little other amusement than in the care of their dependants, and the familiar intercourse of neighbours among whom there was no rivalry or principle of ostentation.

    From all this there resulted, as Madame de L. assures us, a certain innocence and kindliness

This luxuriance of growth does not proceed entirely from the moisture supplied by the ditches and drains; the soil naturally is uncommonly fertile: and whatever springs from it, whether planted by the hand of man, and nourished, while growing, by his attention and skill, or its spontaneous production, bears witness to this uncommon fertility. The country abounds in corn and vineyards; the produce of the latter consists principally in white vines. At the season of the year when I passed through it, the intermixture of the rich and soft yellow of the wheat nearly ripe, with the light green foliage of the vines, produced a most pleasing effect. In Poitou and Anjou, the harvest generally begins about the latter end of June: this year it was late every where, but very abundant. The vineyards had mostly failed.

Le Marais, which is also comprehended within the limits of Le Bocage, is that part of Lower Poitou, adjacent to the sea. There the country is open and flat, and the passes are impracticable during the winter, and very difficult at other seasons of the year. The inhabitants of Le Marais formed a division of the army of the celebrated chief Charette. La Vendee was divided into two circuits; each army had its own, until the junction of the whole under La Roche-Jaquelin, &c; that of Charette occupied the district of Chalans, Machecoul, la Roche Sur Yon, les Sables, a part of the districts of St. Florent, Vehiers, Chollet, Chatillon, la Chataigneraie, a great part of the districts of Clisson, Montaigne, Thouars, Parthenay, and Fontenay-le-peuple. Although the locality of Le Bocage is a perfect contrast to that of le Marais, nature seems to have exerted all her power in forming these two districts into one extensive fortress, capable of opposing every thing to an attack, and presenting so many

of character, joined with great hardihood and gaiety,--which reminds us of Henry IV. and his Bearnois,--and carries with it, perhaps on account of that association, an idea of something more chivalrous and romantic--more honest and unsophisticated, than any thing we expect to meet with in this modern world of artifice and derision. There was great purity of morals accordingly, Mad. de L. informs us, and general cheerfulness and content in all this district;--crimes were never heard of, and lawsuits almost unknown. Though not very well educated, the population was exceedingly devout;--though theirs was a kind of superstitious and traditional devotion, it must he owned, rather than an enlightened or rational faith. They had the greatest veneration for crucifixes and images of their saints, and had no idea of any duty more imperious than that of attending on all the solemnities of religion. They were singularly attached also to their cures, who were almost all born and bred in the country, spoke their *patois*, and shared in all their pastimes and occupations. When a hunting-match was to take place, the clergyman announced it from the pulpit after prayers,--and then took his fowling-piece, and accompanied his congregation to the thicket. It was on behalf of these cures, in fact, that the first disturbances were excited.--***Edin. Rev. for Feb.*** 1816.

means of defence, that it was rarely possible for the enemy to lead a column, or to regulate its movements so as to preserve union in its marches or manoeuvres, dispositions for an attack, or retreat. The positions of the Vendeans could never be understood, or their projects foreseen, in a country where the frequent undulations of land, hedges, trees, and bushes, obstructing the surface, would not admit of seeing fifty paces round; and one of the republican generals, writing to the Convention, thus speaks of Charette's movements. "It is no easy matter to find Charette, particularly to bring him to action. To-day at the head of ten thousand men, the next day wandering with a score of horsemen, it is very rare that one can come up with him. When we believed him to be in our front, he was in our rear. Yesterday he threatened such a post, to-day he is ten leagues from it; more able to avoid than fight us, he almost always disconcerts, and often, without knowing it, all our combinations. He endeavours to surprise us, to carry off our patroles, and to kill our stragglers".

The inhabitants of le Marais and le Bocage for a long period confined themselves to defensive warfare, for which nature seems to have formed their country. The situation of le Marais enabled the brave royalists to receive succours from the English, and to facilitate and protect the debarkation of such as they wished to procure from the North side of the Loire, the coast being flat and easy of access by sea.

The Vendeans, favoured by every natural advantage, had a peculiar tactic which they knew perfectly well how to apply to their position and local circumstances, and adopted a mode of fighting hitherto unknown, and practicable in that country alone. Confident in the superiority which their mode of attack gave them, they never suffered themselves to be anticipated, they never engaged but when and where they pleased. Their dexterity in the use of fire arms was such, that no people, however well skilled in manoeuvring, could make such good use of a gun; the huntsman of Loroux, and the poacher of le Bocage, having been always proverbial as excellent marksmen. It was no unusual thing for the Vendeans when at the plough, to carry with them a musket; and whenever they observed "a blue coat," (as they called the republican soldiers) they stopt their plough, took up their musket, and fired at him; it seldom happened that they missed the object of their vengeance. A melancholy circumstance, connected with this mode of warfare, took place: the son of one of the Vendean farmers, or ploughmen, had been compelled to join the republican army; but having succeeded in escaping, he was hastening, in his republican uniform, to rejoin his relations, when being observed by his father, while at the plough, the latter, unable from the distance to recognize his son, and seeing only the uniform of an enemy, fired and shot him.

Their attacks were always dreadful, sudden, and almost unforeseen, because it was very difficult to reconnoitre or obtain information so as to guard against surprise. Their order of battle was generally in the form of a crescent, their wings being composed of the most expert marksmen, who never fired without taking aim, and seldom ever missed. Their retreat was so precipitate that it was difficult to come up with them, as they dispersed themselves through rough fields, hedges, woods, and bushes, knew all the bye-roads, secret escapes and defiles, and were acquainted with all the obstacles which could obstruct their flight, and the means of avoiding them. Their mode of warfare was according to the locality of the country, well calculated to prolong the struggle and waste the strength of the forces sent to oppose them. In the district of les Sables, intersected by canals, rivulets, and salt marshes, where there were scarcely carriage roads, but chiefly bye-ways, and raised paths, a species of natural fortification was every where formed: this rendered any attack against them dangerous, and consequently it was most favourable for defence, particularly to the inhabitants. The canals are in general from thirty to forty feet wide on the upper extremity of the banks. The Vendean, carrying his musket in a bandoleer, and leaning upon a long pole, leaped from one bank to the other with amazing facility. When the pressure of the enemy would not admit of his doing this, without exposing himself to their fire, he threw himself into a niole, (a kind of small boat,) very flat, and light, and crossed the canal with great rapidity, being always sufficiently shut up to hide himself from his pursuers: but he soon appeared again, and firing at his enemy, again disappeared. The republican soldier to whom this mode of fighting was unknown, was obliged to be continually upon his guard, to march along the shores of the canals, and to follow slowly their circuitous track, supporting at the same time frequent skirmishes, while it took him several hours to traverse a space which the Vendean commonly accomplished in a few minutes.

Among the difficulties which the execution of all military plans met with in La Vendee, the nature and degree of which may be judged of from the local dispositions and the kind of warfare carried on by the royalists, there was one which was invincible, and which singularly retarded the operations of the republicans. Whenever they were desirous of sending an order from head quarters to a division at the distance of twelve or fifteen leagues, the messenger was often obliged to travel fifty or sixty in order to avoid passing through the revolted country. Hence the impossibility of attempting any expedition, however necessary or desirable, which required to be executed without delay. The Vendeans would appear one day at a certain point to the number of several thousand men; measures were concerted for attacking them the next day, but before that arrived they were eight or ten leagues distant from the place where they had showed themselves the day before.

Thus were the republicans exposed to fruitless victories or disastrous checks, which exhausted their men and resources. Masters of the field of battle, they found, says one of their generals, nothing but wooden shoes and some slain, never any arms or ammunition. The Vendean when perceived, would either hide or break his gun, and in surrendering his life, seldom left his weapon. Being well acquainted with the country, and more dexterous than the republicans, they carried scarcely any artillery with them, four or five pieces sufficed for an army of thirty or forty thousand men; these were generally light field pieces. Equally sparing of ammunition, they took but few waggons, one alone served the pieces, as they well knew it was not artillery that would procure them the victory; thence, when the republicans met with any disastrous affair, they lost from twenty to thirty pieces of cannon, and waggons in proportion; whereas when they gained a victory they acquired only two or three pieces of cannon, with scarcely any ammunition.

From this slight sketch of the nature of the country, so disadvantageous to the invaders, and of the mode in which the Vendeans carried on this unfortunate war, our surprise will cease at the determined and protracted resistance made to the republicans by this loyal and brave people. For many years they defended their beloved country, and endured privations, and accumulated miseries, such as human nature has seldom been exposed to. To use the words of a republican general, "A girdle of fire enveloped the revolted country; fire, terror, and death, preceded the march".

But the principal cause of the long resistance of the Vendeans must be sought for in their moral character; they were most honourably distinguished by an inviolable attachment to their party, and unlimited and unshaken confidence in their chiefs; and an earnest, warm, but steady zeal, which supplied the place of discipline.

Their invincible courage, both active and passive, was proof against every kind of danger, fatigue, and want. It has been well observed that "irregular and undisciplined wars are naturally far more prolific of extraordinary incidents, unexpected turns of fortune, and striking displays of individual talent, of vice and virtue, than the more solemn movements of national hostility, where every thing is in a great measure provided and foreseen; and where the inflexible subordination of rank, and the severe exactions of a limited duty not only take away the inducement, but the opportunity for those exaltations of personal feeling and adventure which produce the most lively interest, and lead to the most animating results. In the unconcerted proceedings of an insurgent population, all is experiment and all is passion. The heroic daring of a simple peasant lifts him at once to the rank of a leader, and kindles a general enthusiasm to which all things become possible".

From the operation of these causes the Vendeans were enabled to send forth formidable armies: and such was the confidence of the chiefs in the troops, that they never would have been subdued if they had not lost their leaders in the various hard fought actions, or been deprived of their services by their mutual jealousy. Another circumstance proved equally fatal to them; after the fall of the gallant Lescure, they most imprudently quitted the strong country for the open plains on the left bank of the Loire.

CHAP. VII.

RIVER LOIRE, FROM NANTES TO ANGERS.

The Loire is one of the finest rivers in France; and perhaps there is no river in the world, that equals that part of it, which flows from Angers to Nantes: the breadth of the stream; the islands of wood; the boldness, culture, and richness of its banks, all conspire to render it worthy of this character. As a useful river it is equally celebrated: its banks being bordered by rich and populous cities; and the benefits it renders to industry and commerce being incalculable.

Its stream is so rapid and strong, that in ascending it is generally necessary from Nantes to Angers, to track the barge: this mode of proceeding, though slow, has its advantages; as it gives greater time and opportunity for observing all the various beauties of scenery which present themselves at every turn of the river.

I embarked early in the morning with a favourable breeze from the west: we soon began to be interested, and almost enchanted, with the rich and beautiful scenery, which almost every moment opened to our view in endless variety. This scenery not only pleased the eye and imagination by its beauty, but also excited high and deep interest by the fertility which it displayed. The banks were lined with corn fields, vineyards, or orchards. Occasionally the nature and interest of the prospect were agreeably diversified by the spire of a convent or the turrets of a chateau, rising above gardens or groves, or rich woodlands. At other places there were still more decided marks of population, for villages, country-houses, and farms, caught the eye, and added to the charms by which it was so willingly and powerfully detained.

The whole country on each side is well cultivated. But even this part of France, interesting and beautiful as it is, cannot be traversed without the recollection of the horrors of the revolution breaking in upon, and greatly damping the interest and pleasure derived from the view of the scenery. As we approached the ruined tower of Oudon, it was impossible not to feel a melancholy regret at the scenes of unparalleled bloodshed that took place on the rich and delightful banks of this river during the phrenzy of the revolution. These dreadful recollections assailed us most powerfully as we came in view of Ancenis on the left, and of Saint Florent le Viel to the right. At the latter place we stopped for the night. It was a fine serene evening, the wind had left us, and we were forced to track the shore for some distance before we reached it: just as the sun was setting I made a sketch of its ruined convent on the hill.

After the defeat of the Vendean army, and their retreat across the Loire at this place, says a French writer, "There were seen upon the right bank, following the army, which increased prodigiously, a multitude of bishops, priests, monks, religious persons, old countesses, baronesses, &c. &c. who were carried off by cart-loads, and which did nothing but embarrass the army.[11] There were a great many of them killed at the battle of Mans".

It is said that when the Prince Talmont, with the royalists, crossed over from Saint Florent, under the fire of the republican troops who had taken possession of the heights, they consisted of thirty thousand individuals, but that there were not twenty thousand warriors; among them were five thousand women: arrived in the open country, without warlike stores, they soon wanted provisions. This multitude created a famine wherever it went, and suffered a famine itself. The first unsuccess-

---

11   On gaining the heights of St. Florent, one of the most mournful, and at the same time most magnificent spectacles, burst upon the eye. These heights form a vast semicircle; at the bottom of which a broad bare plain extends to the edge of the water. Near an hundred thousand unhappy souls now blackened over that dreary expanse,--old men, infants and women, mingled, with the half-armed soldiery, caravans, crowded baggage waggons and teams of oxen, all full of despair, impatience, anxiety and terror:--Behind, were the smoke of their burning villages, and the thunder of the hostile artillery;--before, the broad stream of the Loire, divided by a long low island, also covered with the fugitives,--twenty frail barks plying in the stream--and, on the far banks, the disorderly movements of those who had effected the passage, and were waiting there to be rejoined by their companions. Such, Mad. de L. assures us, was the tumult and terror of the scene, and so awful the recollections it inspired, that it can never be effaced from the memory of any of those who beheld it; and that many of its awe-struck spectators have concurred in stating, that it brought forcibly to their imaginations the unspeakable terrors of the great day of judgment.--*Edinb. Rev. No. LI. p. 24.*

ful enterprize produced discouragement, and necessarily the desertion of the army: it diminished two-thirds when it was repulsed at Angers; and when the chiefs, despairing (after the battle of Mans) of not being able to recross the Loire at Ancenis, led back the wrecks of the army to Savenay, it consisted only of fifteen thousand men, half dead with hunger and misery: the major part of these were exterminated by the republicans; the rest dispersed themselves, and from that time all efforts ceased. Prince de Talmont was arrested near Erne, tried at Rennes, and executed at Laval: of the fate of Lescure and the other chiefs, a melancholy catalogue is furnished by Madame de la Roche-Jaquelin.

The wind favoring us the day following, we sailed at break of day, and arrived at Angers at the close of a beautiful evening. The approach to this town, in sailing up the river Mayenne, is highly picturesque; its ancient castle is situated on a high rock overhanging the river; its walls and antique towers, built by the English, have an imposing effect. The town stands in a plain, which, in the distance, being fringed with wood, together with the corn and meadow ground, give it that richness and beauty that characterizes the whole country between Nantes and Angers. The river Mayenne, and a small branch of the Loire, divide the town. It is the chief seat of the province of Maine-et-Loire, formerly the capital of Anjou. It is a large ancient city, with a fine cathedral, a botanical garden, museum, and several manufactories of cottons; one of them in imitation of India handkerchiefs. Here the last effort was made by the Vendeans, whose flight from it was immediately followed by the bloody and disastrous affair of Mans.

I had now passed the provinces of Bretagne and Poitou, as they border the Loire; and, in point of beautiful and romantic scenery, this district can scarcely be surpassed. The left bank of the river, running along the country of Le Bocage, from Nantes to Angers, a distance of seventy-two miles, is a continued range of lofty hills, agreeably diversified with corn lands, and studded with vineyards. The opposite bank is a more flat and variegated country, with pleasant eminences and broad plains, watered by branches of the Loire, which in many parts contains small islands covered with trees. The whole course of this fine river, as the eye sweeps and ranges over its banks, presents at almost every bend the view of villas enriched with gardens, orchards, and vineyards; castles, convents, and villages in ruins! bearing innumerable evidences of the desolating war that has destroyed them.

The religious communities, whose love of scenery and retirement in general led them to prefer the most sequestered valleys, have in these provinces chosen the most elevated and picturesque spots for the erection of their monasteries; and these, notwithstanding their deserted and decaying state, prove the good taste of their ancient possessors, and the skill and industry with which they embellished them. No situations could have been selected more abounding in picturesque combinations of magnificent landscapes.

The pleasure of the traveller in surveying such scenes, cannot but be frequently interrupted, by the recollection of the various atrocities which the inhabitants of these fine provinces committed against each other, and of the immense number of innocent victims that were driven from their abode to perish by famine or the sword.

CHAP. VIII.

SAUMUR TO TOURS--TOURS--TOURS TO BLOIS--ORLEANS--AND ORLEANS TO PARIS.

I hired a small carriage, called a ***patache***, to convey me to Saumur and Tours; it is driven by a postillion with two horses, and is open in front, giving the traveller a better opportunity of viewing the country than in a close vehicle.

The town of Saumur is built on both banks of the Loire, with a handsome stone bridge over it; an ancient castle, built on a high rock, commands the whole town. The road from Angers to this place is a high raised causeway, paved, and runs parallel to the river, within a few paces of its banks, the whole distance. Here we entered into Touraine from the province of Anjou. From Saumur to Tours, the road is like the former. The river Loire is on the right hand, and a flat level country on the left, covered with orchards, groves, and meadows. The road is every where raised so high, that it forms a very steep declivity, with narrow pathways down to the entrance of the cottages and villages, which are most romantically situated,--some in orchards, some amidst vineyards, some in gardens, and others in recesses peeping from between the trees. The fences are fantastically interwoven with wreaths of the vines, which frequently creep up the trunk of a pear or a cherry-tree, and cover the slated roofs of the houses, thereby, from the natural luxuriance and wildness of their spreading branches in the fruit season, answering at once the purposes of utility and ornament; for the slates, retaining the heat, ripen the grape sooner than any other mode of training. The corn was now ripe, and added to the interest and beauty of the scenes; in many of the fields the reapers were at work, and the harvest (which happily for France had not been so abundant for many years) was going on with the assistance of the female peasantry, who on all occasions partake and cheer the labours of the field.

Approaching nearer to Tours, I had a fine view of the bridge, which is esteemed the handsomest in France. Between the branches of the trees, I now and then caught a glimpse of the spires of the church and buildings, encompassed by extensive orchards and groves, and open vales between, varied by vineyards. It was a *jour de fête*, and as I drove through the town the streets were gay with holyday people, and crowded in some places with groups of women and girls, whose cheerful countenances proved the admiration with which they viewed the performances of some mountebanks.[12] Tours is the chief seat of the prefecture of the Indre-et-Loire, formerly the capital of the province of Touraine, and is built on a plain on the bank of the Loire. The houses are of a white stone, and in the principal streets well built and lofty: it is altogether one of the handsomest towns in France. The main street, the rue Royale, can boast of a foot pavement, which is seldom to be met with in this country. The environs of the town are also very beautiful; the luxuriance of the soil, abounding in vines, fruits, and every article of life, has attracted such numbers of English to its vicinity, that Tours may be almost considered an English colony.

Its ancient cathedral is in good preservation, notwithstanding it became a prey to the licentious fanaticism of the republicans.

The hotel Saint Julien, where I resided during my stay, stands upon the cloisters of an ancient abbey; and the church, with its fine Gothic pillars, and chapels, remains a monument of those destructive and desolating times! The side aisles are stalls for horses and cattle, and the centre is a *remise* for carriages and the public diligences which run to this inn! The best hotel is the hotel du Faisan. The vast number of English who keep pouring into all the western provinces of this country, by degrees has affected the markets, and will continue to do so, as long as the rage

12   There is no city in Europe where there are more of these sort of people to be seen than at Paris, on the boulevards and different carrefours. The fondness of the Parisians for shows has existed for ages. In a tariff of Saint Lewis for regulating the duties upon the different articles brought into Paris by the gate of the little Chatelet, it is ordained, (Hist. LVIII. cxxxiii.) that whosoever fetches a monkey into the city for sale, shall pay four deniers; but if the monkey belongs to a merry-andrew, the merry-andrew shall be exempted from paying the duty, as well upon the said monkey as on every thing else he carries along with him, by causing his monkey to play and dance before the collector! Hence is derived the proverb "Payer en monnoie de singe," i.e. to laugh at a man instead of paying him. By another article, it is specified, that jugglers shall likewise be exempt from all imposts, provided they sing a couplet of a song before the toll-gatherer.

for emigration lasts. At Tours, every article is one third dearer than at Nantes, and in proportion as the capital is approached every thing becomes more expensive; yet notwithstanding this, living is, and must ever be, infinitely cheaper than in England.

It certainly is no exaggeration to say, that France is richer in the production of fruits and vegetables than any country in Europe, for in no other can be found so many productions of the same climates of the earth, or a soil more naturally abundant. With the exception of some of the northern provinces, every part of France has wine, and the culture of that delicious fruit which produces it is mentioned in its earliest records. By a happy distribution, those provinces which do not bear the vine, are abundantly supplied with other productions. Normandy and Bretagne abound in the finest fruits; Picardy, and the adjoining provinces, in corn. The riches of Lorraine are in its woods; Touraine has ever been famous for its plums and its pears. The banks of the Loire, and the valleys of Dauphine, are celebrated for the richness of their verdure and vegetation; and the more southern provinces of Languedoc and Provence, partake of the climate and productions of Italy and Spain.

Between Tours and Amboise, I passed the once celebrated Chateau of Chanteloup, formerly the property of the Duc de Choiseuil, now the residence of the Comte de Chaptal, who became the purchaser when it was sold as national property.

At the distance of six miles from Blois, the road leads near enough to Valencay to have a good view of its magnificent palace and grounds; this place, now belonging to M. de Talleyrand, Prince et Duc de Benevento, (one of the most extraordinary characters who have figured so conspicuously during the present age,) is the more interesting, from having been so long the place of confinement of Ferdinand the present King of Spain; and from whence our government tried to extricate him through the agency of Baron de Kolly, who lost his life in the attempt. This singular transaction has appeared in all the public papers, but having had an opportunity of collecting the particulars through a channel of undoubted authority, I consider it an anecdote of too interesting a nature, as connected with the subject before me, not to insert it here.

In 1810, our government laid a plan to liberate King Ferdinand VII. of Spain, similar to the one which had already effected the escape of the Marquis de la Romana. The person entrusted with this commission, assumed the name of Baron de

Kolly, and besides the necessary credit and credentials, he was furnished with the original letter, written by Charles IV. to George III. in 1802, notifying the marriage of his son, the Prince of the Asturias, and containing a marginal note from the Marquis W.... in corroboration of his mission. A small squadron was also sent to cruize off that part of the coast most contiguous to Valencay, under the orders of Commodore C.... to be in readiness to receive the royal fugitive. On a sudden the Baron de Kolly was seized, and the plan frustrated, but the real particulars were never known until after the events of the campaign of 1815.

In the course of the passage to St. Helena, Admiral C.... (who had been entrusted with the project) expressed a wish to know of Buonaparte, by what means de Kolly had been discovered and arrested, and the true circumstances of the affair so totally unknown in England, adding, that if no motive of state policy intervened, he was anxious to hear the whole disclosure. Buonaparte readily consented, and told him that de Kolly arrived at Paris and lived in the greatest obscurity, dressed shabbily, and eating his meals only at cheap traiteurs in the Fauxbourg St. Antoine. However, he was not satisfied with the common wine served up, and would ask for the best Bordeaux, for which he paid five francs per bottle. This contrast of poverty and luxury excited suspicions in the waiters of the two houses he thus frequented, who being in the pay of the police, immediately sent in a report. De Kolly was watched, and soon afterwards seized with all his papers. Buonaparte said he then procured a person, as nearly resembling de Kolly as could be found, to carry on the English stratagem, under a hope that Ferdinand would have fallen into the trap; and with all the original credentials, this agent of the French police went into the castle of Valencay, under a pretext of selling some trinkets. Ferdinand however, said Buonaparte, was too great a coward to enter into the views proposed to him, but instantly gave information of what had been communicated, to his first chamberlain, Amazada, in a letter written to the governor of the castle!--By this means Ferdinand escaped being placed at the mercy of Buonaparte, whose intention was to intercept him in his flight.

Although the conduct of Ferdinand was in this instance pusillanimous and cruel, it was next to an impossibility that he could have effected his escape. He was surrounded by guards and spies of every description, under the superintendence of M. Darberg, Auditor of the Council of State, and without whose leave no admittance could be obtained. Twenty-five horse gendarmes regularly mounted guard about the castle, and every person found in its vicinity without a regular passport, was confined and strictly examined.

At a small distance, is the residence of Marshal Victor, Duc de Belluno, whom I met walking in the grounds. I was very civilly permitted to enter, on sending a message desiring permission, as a traveller, to see it. It stands at the entrance of the village of Menard, and was once the favourite residence of Madame de Pompadour, the mistress of Louis XV. The river Loire winds beautifully beneath the terrace. The grounds are of a vast extent, and tastefully laid out. Over the entrance, the workmen were then placing the arms of the Marshal, finely executed in stone.

The country is thickly enclosed on each side of the river, varied with hill and dale, clothed with vineyards. The villages and small towns along the banks, as far as Orleans, are numerous and invariably picturesque. Nothing can be more beautiful than the natural festoons which are formed by the long shoots of the vines as they project over the road. The peasants and the vignerons live in the midst of their vineyards; their dwellings are excavations in chalky strata of the solid rock, which afford them warm and dry habitations; some of them were so covered with the vines that the entrance was scarcely visible, and the comparison of them to so many birds nests is not badly imagined. The hedges were covered with wild thyme and rosemary; and the clematis interwoven with honeysuckles and other fragrant flowers, richly perfumed the air. The grapes in Touraine and Orleanois are not abundant this year, but the wine that is expected to be made, will, it is supposed, from the dryness of the summer, be of an excellent quality.

The town of Orleans is memorable for the siege it sustained against the English in 1428, when the maid of Orleans acquired so much renown, and whose barbarous execution at Rouen, cannot be remembered without feelings of horror and indignation, and must ever remain a stain on the memory of that brave soldier the Duke of Bedford. The transactions subsequent to that event, led to the almost entire expulsion of the English from France; and those glittering conquests which were an object of more glory than interest, and had been purchased at such an expense of blood and treasure, were from that time lost to the English nation.

During the Revolution, the ancient statue of this celebrated female was taken down and unfortunately destroyed, and one more modern, but less interesting, finely executed in bronze, has been since erected. She is habited in armour, with a lance and shield, supposed to be leading on the victorious troops. At the four angles, are the emblematical figures in relief, of the principal events of her singular career. On a marble pedestal, is inscribed:

A JEANNE D'ARC.

Orleans is the chief seat of the department of the Loiret, formerly the capital of Orleanais, on the river Loire, over which it has a handsome bridge like the one at Tours, though not of such extent, as the river here is not so wide, and very shallow. The communication by water with Paris is carried on by means of a canal.

The church is one of the finest specimens of Gothic architecture I have seen in France. The towers are of open fretwork, and in excellent preservation. More cheerful scenes of exuberant fertility are nowhere to be met with than along the banks of the river, and in the country surrounding the town.

From Orleans to Etampes, there is a plain of eighteen leagues in extent, the whole of which was covered with one entire tract of corn and vines; not an intervening hill or hillock; and the scene was doubly interesting from the harvest carrying on in every direction as I traversed it.

Leaving Etampes, I passed through the beautiful villages of Sceaux, Bourg-la-Reine, and Fontenay-aux-Roses; the latter still contains the ruins of the Palace of Colbert, the celebrated minister of Louis XIV.

The village of Fontenay-aux-Roses, is situated in a valley six miles from Paris, and takes its name from the culture of roses, which cover large tracts of ground. The proprietors sell the flowers to the distillers for making rose water and essences, and the flower market is supplied with the choicest bouquets; it is likewise celebrated for its produce of the finest strawberries and peaches.

The beauty of its situation, and the association of its name with the sweetest of flowers, has attracted many of the wealthy inhabitants of the metropolis to reside in its vicinity, where they have summer houses; among them is the Maire de Fontenay, Monsieur Ledru, whose history is singular and interesting.

His father, who was very wealthy, and a great miser, sent for him one morning, at the time he had just attained his eighteenth year, and said to him: "I began life at your age with half a crown; there is one for you--go, and be as fortunate as I have been;"--saying which, he turned him out of the house, and shut the door in his face.

Undismayed at such unexpected and unnatural conduct on the part of his parent, whom he had never offended, the youth sought the advice and assistance of a friend, by whose opinion he applied himself to the study of medicine. After an indefatigable study at the Hotel Dieu, he became celebrated in his profession, and had the good fortune to be employed by a lady of great wealth, whose life he saved. Out of gratitude, she proposed to become his wife, and to settle upon him an income of fifty thousand livres, that he might give up his medical pursuits; which, having accepted, he rewarded her by an attention and kindness suitable to the noble generosity of her conduct.

The revolution soon after occurred, and in the general wreck of property she lost all her fortune, it having been invested, either in the funds, or public securities. It then became the turn of Mons. Ledru to support his wife, by renewing the practice of his profession, which soon placed them again in affluent circumstances.

At the death of his father, who left an immense fortune to be divided between Mons. Ledru and his two maiden sisters, he took possession of the estate at Fontenay-aux-Roses, from whence he had been cruelly banished when a boy, and which the unkindness of his parent had never after permitted him to enter. Fortune, which had hitherto played a wayward and capricious game with him, had not yet ceased her freaks. In removing a mirror from over a chimney-piece which required an alteration, he discovered a prodigious treasure that had been concealed there by his father! With that generosity and nobleness of character, which make him esteemed and beloved by all his acquaintance, and adored by the whole commune over which he presides, he instantly sent for his sisters and divided it with them. His wife did not long survive this last event, and since her death he has continued to reside at Fontenay-aux-Roses with his sisters, where he exercises his authority with mildness; and by constant acts of beneficence and charity, is justly styled, "Le Pere de Fontenay!"

Between Fontenay-aux-Roses and Paris, to the right of the road, is the village of Gentilly, whose numerous guinguettes are much frequented by the Parisians in fine weather. It being a holyday we met crowds of well dressed citizens, in all sorts of vehicles, driving towards it. An interesting circumstance had been related to me of the cure of this village, M. Detruissart; and on asking permission to visit his rural habitation, I found the story to be true. His garden, which is not above half an acre, has been laid out with such art and ingenuity, as to give an idea of considerable extent, and to add to the charms of this little spot, which he calls his "bonheur," there are a variety of inscriptions of his own composition; over an arbour of vines is the following:--

MA SOLITUDE.

Loin des mechans, du bruit, des tempetes du monde,
Sous un simple berceau dont la treille est feconde,
Sous un modeste toit, dans de rians jardins,
Dessines, eleves, cultives par mes mains....
C'est dans ces lieux cheris que s'ecoule ma vie
Dans une paix profonde, une tranquillite
Qui sans cesse rappele a mon ame ravie
Le temps de l'age d'or et ma felicite:
Mais, quelque doux qu'il soit, mon sort est peu de chose;
Car enfin, apres tout, je dois mourir bientot!
Ne ressemblons-nous pas a la feuille de rose
Qui paroit un instant et qui seche aussitot!

It was in the practice of the moral conveyed by these lines, and in the pursuit of literature, and constant acts of charity, that Mons. Detruissart passed his life, which was rewarded by the esteem and affection of all his parishioners, of which they gave a remarkable proof on the 4th of July, 1815, when the Prussian troops took post at Gentilly, from whence they had driven the French the preceding evening into Paris. The poor cure, with many other of the inhabitants, sought refuge in the capital, leaving his house at the mercy of the enemy, who commenced plundering in all directions; the humble and modest appearance of M. Detruissart's cottage not attracting their notice, it remained untouched, when a single word from any of the inhabitants would have devoted it to ruin; but such was their esteem for him, that at his return he found every thing as he had left it.

I entered Paris, leaving Bicetre to my right, by the barriere d'Enfer, after one of the most agreeable and interesting journeys I ever performed.

CHAP. IX.

ENVIRONS OF PARIS--PERE LA CHAISE--CASTLE OF VINCENNES--
AND CHATEAU OF ST. GERMAIN--ITS FOREST AND VICINITY.

Prior to the revolution, the French, like most other European nations, were in the practice of depositing their dead in churches and cemeteries within the most populous towns, in compliance with those precepts of evangelical doctrine which recommend us unceasingly to reflect on death; and hence originated a custom which cannot but be attended with most pernicious consequences to health, when we reflect that the decomposition of human bodies is productive of putrid exhalations, and consequently pregnant with the causes of contagious disorders. It is indeed surprising that some regulations have not hitherto been adopted in England regarding the interment of the dead, from the example of other countries.

In the year 1793, a decree was passed by the National Assembly, to prevent burying in churches, or in church-yards, within the city of Paris. Since which period, there have been three places selected in its immediate neighbourhood for that purpose--Montmartre, called "Le Champ du Repos"--Vaugirard, and Pere La Chaise.

Quitting the Boulevards, at the extremity of the Boulevards Neufs, eastward of the city, and passing through the Barriere d'Aulnay, I arrived at the Pere La Chaise. At the entrance, through large folding gates, is a spacious court-yard, having at one angle the dwelling of the Concierge, or Keeper. The enclosure contains one hundred and twenty acres, on a gently rising ground, in the centre of which stands the ancient mansion constructed by Louis XIV. for his confessor, Pere la Chaise, the celebrated Jesuit, who, with Madame de Maintenon, governed France. Rising above the thousands of tombs which surround it, it displays itself a wrecked and mouldering monument of ancient splendour, and the mutability of human affairs! This spot became afterwards a place of public promenade and great resort, from the beauty of its position overlooking all Paris; and though so often the scene of festivity and pleasure, now presents to the eye of the beholder a mournfully interesting sight of tombs and sarcophagi, intermixed with various fruit trees, cypress groves, the choicest flowers, and rarest shrubs.

From the rising ground, above the building of Pere La Chaise, a most delightful view displays itself. The city of Paris appears to stand in the centre of a vast amphitheatre. The heights of Belleville, Montmartre, and Menilmontant, in the west. To the east, the beautiful plain of Saint-Mande, Montreuil, and Vincennes, with the lofty towers of its fortress.--The fertile banks of the river Marne, are on the North, and in the South, the horizon encircles Bicetre and Meudon.

The various tombs are placed without order or regularity: they are mostly enclosed with trellis work of wood, sometimes by iron railing; and consist of a small marble column, a pyramid, a sarcophagus, or a single slab, just as may have suited the fancy or the taste of the friends of the departed.--Some surrounded with cypress, some with roses, myrtles, and the choicest exotics; others with evergreens, and not unfrequently a single weeping willow, with the addition of a rose tree!

This intermixture of the sweetest scented flowers and fruit trees, in a burying ground, among the finest pieces of sculptured marble, with evergreens growing over them, in the form of arbours, and furnished with seats, cannot fail to produce in the mind of the person who views it for the first time, peculiar and uncommon feelings of domestic melancholy, mingled with pleasing tenderness.

Who could be otherwise than powerfully affected, as I was, by the first objects that presented themselves to me on entering the place?--A mother and her two sons, kneeling in pious devotion at the foot of the husband's and the father's grave! At a short distance, a female of elegant form, watering and dressing the earth around some plants at her lover's tomb!--not a day, and seldom an hour, passes, but some one is seen either weeping over the remains of a departed relative, or watching with pious solicitude the flowers that spring up around it.

Among the many interesting objects that presented themselves at my first visit, was the tomb of Abelard and Heloise, which had not long since been removed from the convent of the Augustins, where I had seen it in 1815.

At a little distance, to the left of the former, was the burial place of Labedoyere. The fate of this brave and unfortunate officer is well known; his youth, and misled zeal, have procured him a sympathy which his fellow sufferer Marshal Ney did not find, and did not merit.

In the centre of a square plot of ground enclosed with lattice work, is erected a wooden cross, painted black. Neither marble, nor stone, nor letters, indicate his name. Two pots of roses, and a tuft of violets, alone marked the spot, which is carefully weeded. There is something more affecting in all this simplicity, something, in my mind, that goes more directly home to the heart, than in the most splendid monument or the most studied eulogium. As we came suddenly up we saw two females clad in deep mourning, weeping over it; at each arm of the cross was suspended a garland of flowers; we were about to retire again immediately, from the fear of disturbing their melancholy devotions, when the concierge, with a brutality indescribable, rushed forward, and removing the garlands, threw them among the shrubs at a considerable distance. The friend who accompanied me, after searching, recovered one of the garlands, and with more gallantry perhaps than policy, immediately replaced it, and reproaching the keeper with his unmanly conduct, vowed vengeance if he dared to interrupt the ladies, again, when bowing to them we retired.

As we were about to quit the place some time after, we were arrested by two gendarmes, and it was not till after a detention of some hours, and a long discussion between the police officers who had been summoned to attend, and being threatened to be sent to the Conciergerie prison, that we were allowed to depart.

The following words were engraved on a plain marble slab that covered the remains of Marshal Ney.

CI GIT
LE MARECHAL NEY
DUC D'ECHLINGEN
PRINCE DE MOSCOWA
DECEDE le 7, Decembre, 1815.

The grave of the Marshal, as well as that of Labedoyere, when I again visited the spot, had been stripped of every thing, and the railing around them removed so as to prevent any one from discovering the place of their interment.

The monument of Madame Cottin, the author of Elizabeth and of Mathilde, is, like her writings, simple and affecting!-Surrounded by a trellis work in the form of an arbour, planted with rose trees, stands a pillar of the whitest marble, highly polished, inclining forwards, and engraved with:

ICI REPOSE
Marie-Sophie Risteav
Veuve de J.M. Cottin
Decedee le 25 Aout.
1815.

Near this is the tomb of the esteemed and celebrated poet Delille, the "Songster of the Gardens," as the French term him. The monument is enclosed in a small garden, planted with the choicest flowers and shrubs: it is of white marble, of large dimensions, and approached by an *allee verte*. The door leading to the vault is of brass, with emblematical figures in relief: above the entrance is inscribed in letters of gold.

JACQVES-DELILLE.

The linden tree, intermixed with various evergreens, form an interesting and beautiful bouquet around it.

Beyond this, to the right, are the tombs of Gretry the composer, Fourcroy the great chemist, Fontenelle, Boileau, Racine, and of Mademoiselle Raucourt, the celebrated actress, to whom the bigotry of the clergy refused burial in consecrated ground in 1815! a circumstance which gave rise to much clamour and dissatisfaction. It is surprising, that after such events as have been experienced in France, the folly of denying the right of consecrated ground to a comedian should have been persevered in, *after the restoration* of Louis XVIII!

Close to the tomb of Mad'lle Raucourt, is one, which for its affecting simplicity and modesty, struck me very forcibly: in a little garden of roses and lilies, and amidst some tufts of mignonette which appeared to have been newly watered, stood a plain marble column, with the words as represented in the annexed sketch--an accacia shaded it from the sun's rays. In 1814, when the Allies approached Paris, this height, like the others commanding the capital, was fortified, and occupied by the students of the Polytechnical School, who defended it with great gallantry. The walls were perforated with holes for the musketry: the marks are still visible where they have been since filled up. On the 30th of March, 1814, this position was vigorously attacked, with great slaughter on both sides: the assailants and the assailed fell in heaps, and it was not until the chief part of a Prussian corps, (that afterwards carried it by assault) had been annihilated, that the brave youths gave way.

The tomb of my early friend and brother officer, the brave and unfortunate Captain Wright, who was murdered in the Temple, is in the cemetery of Vaugirard. I had searched for it in vain at Pere la Chaise, where it was reported he had been buried. It has on it the following inscription, written to his memory by his companion in arms, and in imprisonment, the gallant Sir Sidney Smith:

HERE LIES INHUMED
JOHN WESLEY WRIGHT,
BY BIRTH AN ENGLISHMAN,
CAPTAIN IN THE BRITISH NAVY

Distinguished both among his own Countrymen and Foreigners
For skill and courage;

To whom,
Of those things which lead to the summit of glory,
Nothing was wanting but opportunity:

His ancestors, whose virtues he inherited,
He honoured by his deeds.

Quick in apprehending his orders,
Active and bold in the execution of them;

In success modest,

In adverse circumstances firm,
In doubtful enterprises, wise and prudent.

Awhile successful in his career;
At length assailed by adverse winds, and on an hostile shore,
He was captured;

And being soon after brought to Paris,
Was confined in the prison called the Temple,
Infamous for midnight murders,
And placed in the most rigid custody:

But in bonds,
And suffering severities still more oppressive,
His fortitude of mind and fidelity to his country
Remained unshaken.

A short time after,
He was found in the morning with his throat cut.
And dead in his bed:

He died the 28th October, 1805, aged 36.
To be lamented by his Country,
Avenged by his God!

THE DONJON, OR CASTLE OF VINCENNES.

This ancient fortress is situate at the entrance of the forest of Vincennes, (now reduced to a wood of small trees, the large timber having been cut down during the revolution) and surrounded by a deep ditch of great width, about two miles from the Barriere du Trone. During many ages, it had been the casual residence of the sovereigns of France. Philip de Valois added considerably to its dimensions in 1337. John continued the works, and during his captivity in England, Charles his son, then regent of the kingdom, finished it.

During the reign of Charles VII. in 1422, Henry VI. of England died in this castle. From this time Vincennes became a royal residence, until the reign of Louis XIV. when that monarch fixed himself at Versailles, from which period it has never been used but as a prison.[13]

Dulaure, a French writer, in speaking of the persons who were confined here, observes, it would be difficult to enumerate the number of individuals that have been shut up in this prison within these few years. "We will merely notice," he says, "the celebrated Count Mirabeau, who was confined from 1777 to 1780; here it was that he translated his Tibulle, and Joannes Secundus, and wrote his 'Lettres originales' to his mistress, Madame Lemonnier, which abound with passages as affecting as the letters of Heloise".

This prison was thrown open during the reign of the unfortunate Louis XVI. by the Baron de Breteuil, Minister of the Department of Paris in 1784. In going over it, every one was penetrated with horror; and feelings of the most melancholy interest were excited by reading the various inscriptions on the walls, indicative of the hopeless misery that had been experienced within them! Many were expressive of piety and resignation at the approach of death!--others complaining of the cruel oppression which had immured them! On one wall was written, "Il faut mourir, mon frere; mon frere il faut mourir, quand il plaira a Dieu". On the door of another prison were, "Beati qui persecutionem patiuntur propter justitiam, quoniam ipsorum est regnum caelorum". On the same spot were, "Carcer Socratis, templum honoris".

This Donjon remained unoccupied until 1791. At this period, the prisons of the capital being filled with criminals, Government ordered it to be prepared for the reception of that class of prisoners; but on the massacres that followed, the mob either murdered or released them all, after a bloody contest, and it remained again

---

13   Monstrelet relates a curious anecdote, during the residence at the Castle of Vincennes of Isabeau de Baviere, strongly illustrative of the barbarous manners of those times. "Lewis de Bourbon, who was handsome and well made, and had signalized himself upon various occasions, and amongst others at the battle of Agincourt, going one night, as was customary, to visit the Queen, Isabeau de Baviere, at the Castle of Vincennes, met the King (Charles VI.); he saluted him, without either stopping or alighting from his horse, but continued galloping on. The King having recollected him, ordered Tangui du Chatel, prevost of Paris, to pursue, and to confine him in prison. At night the *question* was applied, and he was afterwards tied up in a sack and cast into the Seine, with this inscription upon the sack, 'Let the King's justice take place.'"

without prisoners until the Imperial Government under Buonaparte. It was then garrisoned by a detachment of the Imperial Guard, and multitudes of victims were transferred there whose fate remains, and probably ever will remain, unknown.

It was to this place that the Duke D'Enghien, who was arrested the 15th March, 1804, at Ettenheim, in the Electorate of Baden, was conducted the 20th of the same month, at five in the evening, and condemned to death the night following, by a military commission, at which Murat presided. He was accordingly shot on the 21st, at half past four in the evening, in the ditch of the castle which looks towards the forest, on the north side, and his body thrown into a grave, ready dug to receive it, where he fell. The details of this cruel and wanton act of barbarity are too well known to need any repetition here.

This spot is now marked by a wooden cross, enclosed by an iron railing. The remains of the Prince were dug out on the 20th March, 1816, by order of Louis XVIII. and deposited with solemn funeral ceremony in a coffin which is placed in the same apartment where the council of war condemned him to suffer! since transformed info a chapel. Under a cenotaph, covered with a cloth of gold, is placed the coffin, with a prodigious large stone lying on it, the same that was found lying on his head, and which from its weight had crushed his skull!

The apartment is hung with black cloth, and remains continually lighted, with a guard placed over it. Mass is daily performed for the repose of his soul, agreeable to the Catholic religion.

On the lid of the coffin is the following inscription:

Ici est Le Corps
De Tres-Haut, Tres-Puissant Prince
Louis-Antoine-Henri De Bourbon
Duc D'Enghien, Prince du Sang
Pair de France
Mort A Vincennes, Le 21 Mars 1804
A L'age de XXXI Ans VII mois XVIII Jours.
A marble bust of the Prince, by Bosio, is placed at the entrance.

During the periods of 1814 and 1815, when Paris was in possession of the Allies, Vincennes continued under the command of General Daumesnil, who declared that he held it for his country until the Government was settled, and would not open its gates to a foreign army. It was not attacked either of the times.

It is approached by two gates, with drawbridges, and defended by cannon on all sides. The fosse is of great depth, and dry, extending, I should suppose, nearly a quarter of a mile. It has nine towers, of prodigious height and solidity: the largest, at the south western angle, called the Donjon, is considerably more elevated than the others. The principal entrance is fronting the forest, on the north side, in the form of a triumphal arch, with six pillars, ornamented in bas-reliefs, and was decorated with marble statues, which were destroyed when it was seized by the mob.

The Donjon is surrounded by a separate ditch, within the other, of forty feet depth, and is approached by two draw-bridges; one for carriages, the other for foot passengers; and the main tower is flanked by four other angular ones, each having a high turret. The windows are treble barred within and without, so as to admit but a faint glimmering light! Three gates of great solidity are to be passed at the entrance; that which communicates with the draw-bridge of the castle is secured both within and without. After passing the three gates, there is a court, in the middle of which stands the Donjon. Three other immense gates guard its entrance!

The form of the Donjon is a square. The towers at the four angles are divided into five floors, each having a separate stair-case, and each floor is vaulted, with an apartment in the centre, sustained by pillars, which are chimneys. At each of the four corners of the apartment in the centre is a cell thirteen feet square. The towers are encompassed on the third story by a large gallery on the outside, and on the top of each there is a small circular terrace. Such is the strength and prodigious solidity of this building, that it is said to be capable of resisting the heaviest cannon, and is bomb proof. The hand of time appears not to have made any impression on its outward surface.

The first hall is called "La chambre de la question:" its name indicates sufficiently the horrid purposes to which it was appropriated! So late as the year 1790 were to be seen chairs formed of stone, where the unhappy victims were seated, with iron collars fixed to the wall by heavy chains, that confined them to the spot while undergoing the torture! In these prisons, deprived of air and light, were beds of timber, on which they were allowed to repose during the interval of their sufferings.

The upper floor, named "La salle du conseil," from the Kings holding their council there, while it was a royal residence, is secured by a door of great solidity, and each prison at the angles had three doors covered with iron plates, with double locks and treble bolts. The doors were so contrived as to open crossways, each serving as a security to the other. The first acted as a bar to the second, and this to the third, so that it was necessary to close one before the other could be opened.--Such was the mode of confinement in this prison, the walls of which are sixteen feet thick, and the arches thirty feet high.

The other eight towers were also prisons. The one called "La tour de la surintendance" contains cells six feet square; the bed places are of stone. There is a square hole to descend into the vaults beneath, where, like a tomb, the miserable prisoner was immured for ever!!! Often, alas! for imaginary crimes, or for causes which make us shudder at their wantonness and barbarity, an unfortunate victim has been torn from the bosom of his family, to perish unheard of and unknown!

The French Government have, I understand, issued an order to prevent any one from entering this place from motives of curiosity; and let us hope that the humane and enlightened policy of the restored Monarch will close its cells for ever!

The following beautiful lines, with which I close an account of the most horribly interesting spot I ever visited, are from the pen of Delille:

"........................
Voyez gemir en proie a sa longue torture,
Ce mortel confine dans sa noire cloture.
Pour unique plaisir et pour seul passe-temps,
De sa lente journee il compte les instans,
Ou de son noir cachot mesure l'etendue,
Ou medite en secret sa fuite inattendue;
Ou, de ceux qu'avant lui renferma la prison,
Lit, sur ces tristes murs, la complainte et le nom:
Et lui-meme y tracant sa douloureuse histoire,
A ceux qui le suivront en transmet la memoire.
C'est peu d'etre enchaine dans ces tristes tombeaux,

Combien de souvenirs viennent aigrir ses maux!
Helas! tandis qu'aupres de leurs jeunes compagnes;
Dans les riches cites, dans les vastes campagnes;
Ses amis d'autrefois errent en liberte,
Lorsque l'heure propice a la societe,
Reconduit chaque soir la jeunesse folatre
Aux entretiens joyeux, a la danse, au theatre,
Ou, d'un plaisir plus doux annoncant le retour,
Du moment fortune vient avertir l'amour,
Il est seul; ... en un long et lugubre silence,
Pour lui le jour s'acheve, et le jour recommence;
Il n'entend point l'accent de la tendre amitie,
Il ne voit point les pleurs de la douce pitie:
N'ayant de mouvement que pour trainer des chanes,
Un coeur que pour l'ennui, des sens que pour les peines,
Pour lui, plus de beaux jours, de ruisseau, de gazon;
Cette voute est son ciel, ces murs son horizon,
Son regard, eleve vers les flambeaux celestes,
Vient mourir dans la nuit de ses cachots funestes;
Rien n'egaie a ses yeux leur morne obscurite;
Ou si, par des barreaux avares de clarte,
Un faible jour se glisse en ces antres funebres,
Il redouble pour lui les horreurs des tenebres,
Et, le coeur consume d'un regret sans espoir,
Il cherche la lumiere et gemit de la voir."

DELILLE. CHATEAU DE SAINT GERMAIN.

This ancient pile of building is now a barrack for the King's Gardes du Corps, containing two troops, one of Luxembourg, and the other of Grammont, which are relieved every three months.

It is supposed to have been built in the reign of Robert, but there appears to be no certainty as to the exact period. It is interesting to the English traveller, from having been the last refuge of James the Second of England, and the residence, at various times, of very celebrated and distinguished characters. It was taken, and pillaged, and partly burnt, during the reign of Philip VI, in 1346, by Edward the Third, and again by the English in 1419, and rebuilt by Francis the First. During the war of the League in 1574, Catherine de Medicis retired to this Castle, but from the predictions of an astrologer, that she would die there, quitted it shortly after, and returned to the Tuilleries, which Palace she had founded.[14] Henry the Fourth often frequented Saint Germain. The Chateau Neuf, and one of the towers, called Le Pavilion de Gabrielle, which is still in good preservation, were erected by him, close to the Castle, for the residence of his favourite, La belle Gabrielle:[15] and the superb terrace was begun in his reign. From this spot the view is very interesting and extensive: nothing can surpass the admirable assemblage of hills, meadows, gardens, and vineyards, which charm the eye, and which as they are viewed from its different points on a clear summer's evening, appear at every turn, in new beauty, and endless variety.

---

14   According to Mezeray, this palace had its name from the spot whereon it is situated, which was called Les Tuilleries, because tiles (des tuiles) were made here. Catherine de Medicis built it 1564. It consisted of nothing but the large square pavilion in the middle, the two wings, and the two pavilions which terminate the wings. Henry IV. Louis XIII. and Louis XIV. afterwards extended, elevated, and embellished it. It is said to be neither so well proportioned, so beautiful, or so regular, as it was at first. The Tuilleries is, nevertheless, a very splendid palace. An astrologer having predicted to Catherine de Medicis, that she would die near St. Germain, she immediately flew, in a most superstitious manner, from all places and churches that bore this name; she no more resorted to St. Germain-en-Laye, and because her palace of the Tuilleries was situated in the parish of Saint Germain l'Auxerrois, she was at the expense of building another, which was the Hotel de Soissons, near the church of St. Eustache. When it was known to be Laurence de Saint Germain, Bishop of Nazareth, who had attended her upon her death-bed, people infatuated with astrology averred that the prediction had been accomplished.

15   Henri IV se plaisait beaucoup a Saint-Germain, et y vint souvent, quand son coeur fut epris des charmes de la belle Gabrielle. Ce prince galant et liberal, qui deja lui avait prouve son amour par le don d'une infinite de maisons de campagne, aux environs de Paris, voulut encore lui donner une preuve de sa tendresse, en batissant pour elle, a deux cents toises de l'ancien chateau, une nouvelle et belle habitation, qu'on appela le Chateau Neuf. Eleve sur les dessins de l'architecte Marchand, il etait surtout remarquable par son architecture simple, ses nombreuses devises, les chiffres amoureux et les emblemes allegoriques qui le decoroient, et qui faisoient une ingenieuse allusion a la passion du monarque pour sa maitresse. L'une des ailes de ce chateau s'appelait meme le Pavillon de Gabrielle.--*Hist. Topo. des Environs de Paris*.

The City of Paris is seen in the distance. The fine aqueduct of Marly, the mountain de Coeur volant, Mount Calvary,[16] and Malmaison to the right; in front the forest of Vesinet, and beyond it the vale of Saint Denis; on the left the hills which encompass the beautiful vale of Montmorency; the Seine winding at the foot, and extending its course until it loses itself in the distance--all within one sweep of the eye!--Such is the enchanting prospect which presents itself.

It was at different times the residence of Louis XIII.[17] of Anne of Austria, Christiana of Sweden, and of Madame La Valiere, when Madame de Montespan rivalled her in the affections of Louis XIV. After the former had retired to the Convent of the Carmelites at Paris, it was assigned in 1689 to the unfortunate James the Second, whose bigotry had driven him from the throne of England. Here, together with his Queen, and those of his court who fled with him to seek an asylum in France, and surrounded by those priests and monks, whose pernicious councils had led to his fall, the unhappy James remained until his death, the 16th Sept. 1701. The apartment in which he breathed his last is still preserved; but the whole of the interior has been very much neglected. It served as a quarter for a body of Prussians in 1815, and the following year was a barrack for the English troops quartered at St. Germain. A French poet of his time wrote these lines descriptive of the life he led in his retirement.

---

16   On the top of this height is the Pavilion de Lucienne, built by Madame Dubarry, Mistress to Louis XV. afterwards the property of Madame La Princesse de Conti, now the residence of M. de Puy: at the foot is the village of Lucienne, surrounded by numerous villas: among the most remarkable is the residence of General Comte Campon.

17   Lewis XIV. would not reside here, because the steeples of the Abbey of St. Denis, where he was to be interred, could be seen from the Chateau. The amount of the immense treasure which the consequent erection of the Palace of Versailles cost was never known, the King Mary Stewart, daughter of James, died here in April 1712, and his Queen, in May 1718. These were the last persons of any consequence who inhabited this palace, which in its exterior still preserves all its ancient appearance of grandeur. It is built of stone, with a facing of red brick, the windows are of great height, and the whole is surrounded by a deep ditch, forming a very striking contrast to the buildings of the present age, having destroyed the bills with his own hand. In the neighbourhood of Versailles stands the celebrated Military School of St. Cyr, which was originally an establishment for the gratuitous admission of two hundred and fifty young ladies of rank, who were to receive an education correspondent to their situation in life. Madame de Maintenon is buried in the Chapel of the Convent.

"C'est ici que Jacques second,
Sans Ministres et sans maitresse,
Le matin allait a la Messe,
Et le soir allait au sermon".

FOREST OF SAINT GERMAIN.

This forest is enclosed by a wall of thirty miles in circumference, according to M. Prudhomme. It is now preserved exclusively for the Duc de Berri, who is the Ranger.

Of all the ancient forests with which Paris is surrounded, this is the most extensive. It is stocked with prodigious quantities of game, with deer, and wild boar. The pheasants and partridges are reared in an extensive *faisanderie*, in the centre of the forest, enclosed by a high wall, and such vigilance is exercised by the keepers, that no person can possibly destroy the game. It is guarded by a captain and two lieutenants, who have under them a corps of gardes de chasse.

The royal chace is, at the commencement of the season, quite a state ceremony, at which all the royal family and the court assemble to be spectators. The dress of the hunt is green and gold, with gold laced cocked hats and swords. The Duke invites his party, and gives them permission to wear the uniform, which is considered a high honour.

Nothing can be more delightful than the walks and rides through this forest; the roads are kept in the best possible state. At intervals are large open spaces called Etoiles, from whence branch off sometimes ten and twelve roads with direction posts, each bearing a separate name, either from some memorable event, or remarkable person; as the croix de Poissy, croix de la Pucelle, croix de Montchevreuil, croix de Berri, and croix de Noailles, &c. &c.

A story is related of a lamentable occurrence which took place the 7th June 1812, at the Etoile des Marres, and a similar one happened in August this year, near the same spot.

The first of these events was occasioned by the parents of a young lady having refused their consent to her being married to her lover, whose want of fortune was the chief obstacle. The lovers, in despair, came to the fatal resolution of putting a period to their lives, and this forest was fixed upon as the spot for the dreadful deed! Having partaken of a repast which they had brought with them, and sworn to love each other (if it were permitted them) after death, they discharged, at the same moment, their pistols at themselves. The unhappy girl fell dead, but the hand of her lover having missed its aim, he was only wounded. Having no other means left of accomplishing his dreadful purpose, he took the handkerchief from her bosom and suspended himself by it to a tree. In this state they were discovered, and their bodies deposited in the same grave! The other circumstance was of the same romantic and melancholy nature.[18] This forest supplies Paris with great quantities of wood.

---

18   There never was known in this country so many fatal instances of suicide as at the present period; few days pass over without some persons throwing themselves out of their windows, or into the river Seine; and among the disappointed partizans of the late ruler, it has been usual to hurl themselves from the top of the column in the Place Vendome, which has been shut up in consequence by an order from Government.

Among the instances of deliberate self-destruction, the following is a remarkable fact, inasmuch as it serves to prove the pernicious effects of the writings of Voltaire and Rousseau in the minds of youth, when at an age incapable of discriminating between fanaticism and real piety!

The person in question was a youth not turned sixteen, who destroyed himself last summer, while at college, and who left the following paper as his last will. The lady who gave it me copied it from the original.

"Testament de Villemain.

"Samedi. July 6th, 1816.

"Je donne mon corps aux Pedants: je legue mon ame aux manes de

Voltaire et de J.J. Rousseau, qui m'ont appris a mepriser toutes les vaines superstitions de ce monde, et tous les vains prejuges qu'a enfantes la grossierete des hommes, et surtout les subtiles noirceurs des fourbes de Pretres.

"J'ai toujours reconnu un Etre supreme, et ma religion a toujours ete la religion naturelle.

"Quant a mes biens terrestres, je donne: (Here he mentions various articles to his favorite school-fellows).

In 1814, and in 1815, the palisades that were made to surround Paris for its defence against the Allied armies, were cut in this wood, and the large timber has consequently been greatly thinned.

Here conclude my notes, and if my reader has condescended to accompany me through my little Tour without feeling fatigue or displeasure at his "Compagnon de Voyage," my aim and ambition as an author are satisfied--so wishing that all the journeys he may ever take, may prove as delightful to him as this has been to me, I sincerely thank him for his attention, and kindly bid him Farewell!

"A Mondesir, mon dernier soupir.

"J'ai toujours connu, je l'ai dit plus haut, reconnu un Etre supreme, j'ai toujours pense que la seul religion digne de lui, etait la vertu et la probite!

"J'ose dire que je m'en suis rarement ecarte malgre la faiblesse, et la fragilite humaine.

.

"Je parois devant l'Etre supreme en disant avec Voltaire: 'Un Bonze, honnete homme, un Dervis, charitable, trouveront plutot grace a ses yeux, qu'un Pontife ambitieux.'"

Then follows a Latin quotation, "All things are due to death, and without delay, sooner or later, hasten to the same goal: Hither we all tend: This is our last asylum".

"De tout les Pedants qui m'ont le plus tourmente je compte surtout Poir, son Jeannes et Veissier, qui sont la cause du vol que je fais a la nature en tranchant moi meme le fil de mes jours; je leur pardonne, l'equite le fait aussi: Je n'ai cesse de repeter avec Rousseau avant de mourir. 'Tu veux cesser de vivre, sais-tu si tu as commence.'

"Adieu!!! Mortels et foiblesses! VILLEMAIN".

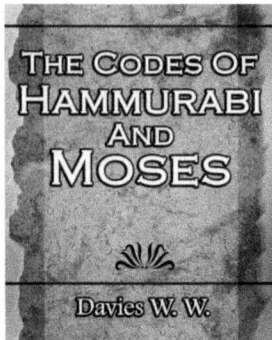

The Codes Of Hammurabi And Moses
W. W. Davies

The discovery of the Hammurabi Code is one of the greatest achievements of archaeology, and is of paramount interest, not only to the student of the Bible, but also to all those interested in ancient history...

Religion   ISBN: *1-59462-338-4*

QTY

Pages:132
MSRP $12.95

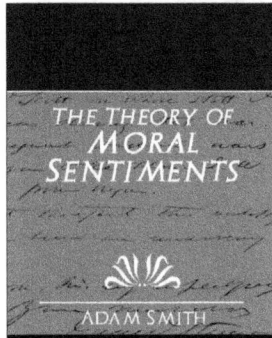

The Theory of Moral Sentiments
Adam Smith

This work from 1749. contains original theories of conscience amd moral judgment and it is the foundation for systemof morals.

Philosophy ISBN: *1-59462-777-0*

QTY

Pages:536
MSRP $19.95

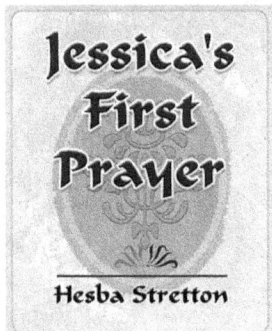

Jessica's First Prayer
Hesba Stretton

In a screened and secluded corner of one of the many railway-bridges which span the streets of London there could be seen a few years ago, from five o'clock every morning until half past eight, a tidily set-out coffee-stall, consisting of a trestle and board, upon which stood two large tin cans, with a small fire of charcoal burning under each so as to keep the coffee boiling during the early hours of the morning when the work-people were thronging into the city on their way to their daily toil...

QTY

Pages:84

Childrens   ISBN: *1-59462-373-2*

MSRP $9.95

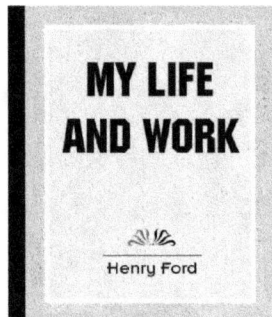

My Life and Work
Henry Ford

Henry Ford revolutionized the world with his implementation of mass production for the Model T automobile. Gain valuable business insight into his life and work with his own auto-biography... "We have only started on our development of our country we have not as yet, with all our talk of wonderful progress, done more than scratch the surface. The progress has been wonderful enough but..."

QTY

Pages:300

Biographies/   ISBN: *1-59462-198-5*

MSRP $21.95

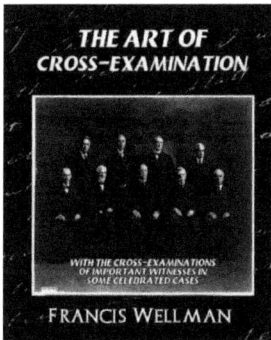

The Art of Cross-Examination
Francis Wellman

QTY

I presume it is the experience of every author, after his first book is published upon an important subject, to be almost overwhelmed with a wealth of ideas and illustrations which could readily have been included in his book, and which to his own mind, at least, seem to make a second edition inevitable. Such certainly was the case with me; and when the first edition had reached its sixth impression in five months, I rejoiced to learn that it seemed to my publishers that the book had met with a sufficiently favorable reception to justify a second and considerably enlarged edition. ..

Pages:412

Reference   ISBN: *1-59462-647-2*   *MSRP $19.95*

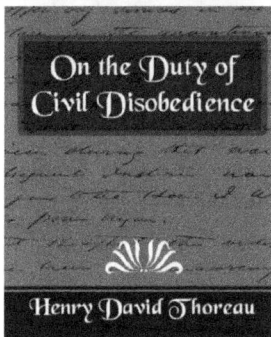

On the Duty of Civil Disobedience
Henry David Thoreau

QTY

Thoreau wrote his famous essay, On the Duty of Civil Disobedience, as a protest against an unjust but popular war and the immoral but popular institution of slave-owning. He did more than write—he declined to pay his taxes, and was hauled off to gaol in consequence. Who can say how much this refusal of his hastened the end of the war and of slavery ?

Law   ISBN: *1-59462-747-9*   **Pages:48**

MSRP $7.45

Dream Psychology Psychoanalysis for Beginners
Sigmund Freud

QTY

Sigmund Freud, born Sigismund Schlomo Freud (May 6, 1856 - September 23, 1939), was a Jewish-Austrian neurologist and psychiatrist who co-founded the psychoanalytic school of psychology. Freud is best known for his theories of the unconscious mind, especially involving the mechanism of repression; his redefinition of sexual desire as mobile and directed towards a wide variety of objects; and his therapeutic techniques, especially his understanding of transference in the therapeutic relationship and the presumed value of dreams as sources of insight into unconscious desires.

Pages:196

Psychology   ISBN: *1-59462-905-6*   *MSRP $15.45*

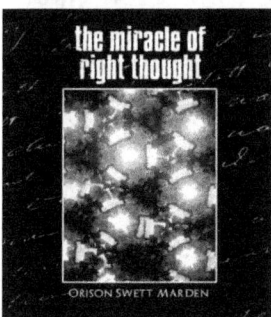

The Miracle of Right Thought
Orison Swett Marden

QTY

Believe with all of your heart that you will do what you were made to do. When the mind has once formed the habit of holding cheerful, happy, prosperous pictures, it will not be easy to form the opposite habit. It does not matter how improbable or how far away this realization may see, or how dark the prospects may be, if we visualize them as best we can, as vividly as possible, hold tenaciously to them and vigorously struggle to attain them, they will gradually become actualized, realized in the life. But a desire, a longing without endeavor, a yearning abandoned or held indifferently will vanish without realization.

Pages:360

Self Help   ISBN: *1-59462-644-8*   *MSRP $25.45*

QTY

The Rosicrucian Cosmo-Conception Mystic Christianity *by Max Heindel* ISBN: *1-59462-188-8* **$38.95**
The Rosicrucian Cosmo-conception is not dogmatic, neither does it appeal to any other authority than the reason of the student. It is: not controversial, but is: sent forth in the, hope that it may help to clear... New Age/Religion Pages 646

Abandonment To Divine Providence *by Jean-Pierre de Caussade* ISBN: *1-59462-228-0* **$25.95**
"The Rev. Jean Pierre de Caussade was one of the most remarkable spiritual writers of the Society of Jesus in France in the 18th Century. His death took place at Toulouse in 1751. His works have gone through many editions and have been republished... Inspirational/Religion Pages 400

Mental Chemistry *by Charles Haanel* ISBN: *1-59462-192-6* **$23.95**
Mental Chemistry allows the change of material conditions by combining and appropriately utilizing the power of the mind. Much like applied chemistry creates something new and unique out of careful combinations of chemicals the mastery of mental chemistry... New Age Pages 354

The Letters of Robert Browning and Elizabeth Barret Barrett 1845-1846 vol II ISBN: *1-59462-193-4* **$35.95**
by Robert Browning and Elizabeth Barrett Biographies Pages 596

Gleanings In Genesis (volume I) *by Arthur W. Pink* ISBN: *1-59462-130-6* **$27.45**
Appropriately has Genesis been termed "the seed plot of the Bible" for in it we have, in germ form, almost all of the great doctrines which are afterwards fully developed in the books of Scripture which follow... Religion/Inspirational Pages 420

The Master Key *by L. W. de Laurence* ISBN: *1-59462-001-6* **$30.95**
In no branch of human knowledge has there been a more lively increase of the spirit of research during the past few years than in the study of Psychology, Concentration and Mental Discipline. The requests for authentic lessons in Thought Control, Mental Discipline and... New Age/Business Pages 422

The Lesser Key Of Solomon Goetia *by L. W. de Laurence* ISBN: *1-59462-092-X* **$9.95**
This translation of the first book of the "Lernegton" which is now for the first time made accessible to students of Talismanic Magic was done, after careful collation and edition, from numerous Ancient Manuscripts in Hebrew, Latin, and French... New Age/Occult Pages 92

Rubaiyat Of Omar Khayyam *by Edward Fitzgerald* ISBN:*1-59462-332-5* **$13.95**
Edward Fitzgerald, whom the world has already learned, in spite of his own efforts to remain within the shadow of anonymity, to look upon as one of the rarest poets of the century, was born at Bredfield, in Suffolk, on the 31st of March, 1809. He was the third son of John Purcell... Music Pages 172

Ancient Law *by Henry Maine* ISBN: *1-59462-128-4* **$29.95**
The chief object of the following pages is to indicate some of the earliest ideas of mankind, as they are reflected in Ancient Law, and to point out the relation of those ideas to modern thought. Religion/History Pages 452

Far-Away Stories *by William J. Locke* ISBN: *1-59462-129-2* **$19.45**
"Good wine needs no bush, but a collection of mixed vintages does. And this book is just such a collection. Some of the stories I do not want to remain buried for ever in the museum files of dead magazine-numbers an author's not unpardonable vanity..." Fiction Pages 272

Life of David Crockett *by David Crockett* ISBN: *1-59462-250-7* **$27.45**
"Colonel David Crockett was one of the most remarkable men of the times in which he lived. Born in humble life, but gifted with a strong will, an indomitable courage, and unremitting perseverance... Biographies/New Age Pages 424

Lip-Reading *by Edward Nitchie* ISBN: *1-59462-206-X* **$25.95**
Edward B. Nitchie, founder of the New York School for the Hard of Hearing, now the Nitchie School of Lip-Reading, Inc, wrote "LIP-READING Principles and Practice". The development and perfecting of this meritorious work on lip-reading was an undertaking... How-to Pages 400

A Handbook of Suggestive Therapeutics, Applied Hypnotism, Psychic Science ISBN: *1-59462-214-0* **$24.95**
by Henry Munro Health/New Age/Health/Self-help Pages 376

A Doll's House: and Two Other Plays *by Henrik Ibsen* ISBN: *1-59462-112-8* **$19.95**
Henrik Ibsen created this classic when in revolutionary 1848 Rome. Introducing some striking concepts in playwriting for the realist genre, this play has been studied the world over. Fiction/Classics/Plays 308

The Light of Asia *by sir Edwin Arnold* ISBN: *1-59462-204-3* **$13.95**
In this poetic masterpiece, Edwin Arnold describes the life and teachings of Buddha. The man who was to become known as Buddha to the world was born as Prince Gautama of India but he rejected the worldly riches and abandoned the reigns of power when... Religion/History/Biographies Pages 170

The Complete Works of Guy de Maupassant *by Guy de Maupassant* ISBN: *1-59462-157-8* **$16.95**
"For days and days, nights and nights, I had dreamed of that first kiss which was to consecrate our engagement, and I knew not on what spot I should put my lips..." Fiction/Classics Pages 240

The Art of Cross-Examination *by Francis L. Wellman* ISBN: *1-59462-309-0* **$26.95**
Written by a renowned trial lawyer, Wellman imparts his experience and uses case studies to explain how to use psychology to extract desired information through questioning. How-to/Science/Reference Pages 408

Answered or Unanswered? *by Louisa Vaughan* ISBN: *1-59462-248-5* **$10.95**
Miracles of Faith in China Religion Pages 112

The Edinburgh Lectures on Mental Science (1909) *by Thomas* ISBN: *1-59462-008-3* **$11.95**
This book contains the substance of a course of lectures recently given by the writer in the Queen Street Hail, Edinburgh. Its purpose is to indicate the Natural Principles governing the relation between Mental Action and Material Conditions... New Age/Psychology Pages 148

Ayesha *by H. Rider Haggard* ISBN: *1-59462-301-5* **$24.95**
Verily and indeed it is the unexpected that happens! Probably if there was one person upon the earth from whom the Editor of this, and of a certain previous history, did not expect to hear again... Classics Pages 380

Ayala's Angel *by Anthony Trollope* ISBN: *1-59462-352-X* **$29.95**
The two girls were both pretty, but Lucy who was twenty-one who supposed to be simple and comparatively unattractive, whereas Ayala was credited, as her Bombwhat romantic name might show, with poetic charm and a taste for romance. Ayala when her father died was nineteen... Fiction Pages 484

The American Commonwealth *by James Bryce* ISBN: *1-59462-286-8* **$34.45**
An interpretation of American democratic political theory. It examines political mechanics and society from the perspective of Scotsman James Bryce Politics Pages 572

Stories of the Pilgrims *by Margaret P. Pumphrey* ISBN: *1-59462-116-0* **$17.95**
This book explores pilgrims religious oppression in England as well as their escape to Holland and eventual crossing to America on the Mayflower, and their early days in New England... History Pages 268

QTY

The Fasting Cure *by Sinclair Upton*   ISBN: *1-59462-222-1*   **$13.95**

In the Cosmopolitan Magazine for May, 1910, and in the Contemporary Review (London) for April, 1910, I published an article dealing with my experiences in fasting. I have written a great many magazine articles, but never one which attracted so much attention... New Age/Self Help/Health Pages 164

Hebrew Astrology *by Sepharial*   ISBN: *1-59462-308-2*   **$13.45**

In these days of advanced thinking it is a matter of common observation that we have left many of the old landmarks behind and that we are now pressing forward to greater heights and to a wider horizon than that which represented the mind-content of our progenitors... Astrology Pages 144

Thought Vibration or The Law of Attraction in the Thought World   ISBN: *1-59462-127-6*   **$12.95**

by William Walker Atkinson   *Psychology/Religion Pages 144*

Optimism *by Helen Keller*   ISBN: *1-59462-108-X*   **$15.95**

Helen Keller was blind, deaf, and mute since 19 months old, yet famously learned how to overcome these handicaps, communicate with the world, and spread her lectures promoting optimism. An inspiring read for everyone... Biographies/Inspirational Pages 84

Sara Crewe *by Frances Burnett*   ISBN: *1-59462-360-0*   **$9.45**

In the first place, Miss Minchin lived in London. Her home was a large, dull, tall one, in a large, dull square, where all the houses were alike, and all the sparrows were alike, and where all the door-knockers made the same heavy sound... Childrens/Classic Pages 88

The Autobiography of Benjamin Franklin *by Benjamin Franklin*   ISBN: *1-59462-135-7*   **$24.95**

The Autobiography of Benjamin Franklin has probably been more extensively read than any other American historical work, and no other book of its kind has had such ups and downs of fortune. Franklin lived for many years in England, where he was agent... Biographies/History Pages 332

Name	
Email	
Telephone	
Address	
City, State ZIP	

☐ **Credit Card**   ☐ **Check / Money Order**

Credit Card Number	
Expiration Date	
Signature	

Please Mail to: Book Jungle
PO Box 2226
Champaign, IL 61825
or Fax to: 630-214-0564

ORDERING INFORMATION

web: *www.bookjungle.com*
email: *sales@bookjungle.com*
fax: *630-214-0564*
mail: *Book Jungle PO Box 2226 Champaign, IL 61825*
or PayPal *to sales@bookjungle.com*

Please contact us for bulk discounts

DIRECT-ORDER TERMS

**20% Discount if You Order
Two or More Books**
Free Domestic Shipping!
Accepted: Master Card, Visa,
Discover, American Express

www.ingramcontent.com/pod-product-compliance
Lightning Source LLC
LaVergne TN
LVHW081325060426
835511LV00011B/1863